TITANIC STYLE

For Charlotte and Emilia

TITANIC STYLE

Dress and Fashion on the Voyage

Grace Evans

SKYHORSE PUBLISHING
A HERMAN GRAF BOOK

Contents

1. Introduction

THE STORY OF THE TITANIC, her construction, opulence, and tragic loss on her maiden voyage captured public imagination from the very start. The first and strongest reaction was naturally shock at the sheer number of people lost, but this quickly developed into fascination with the human stories that lay behind the stark statistics. The individual experiences of those on board, survivors or victims, crew or passengers, soon began to emerge. They told of tragedy, but also revealed tales of great heroism, luck and survival, providing a permanent bittersweet backdrop that colours all exploration of the phenomenon of the *Titanic*.

RMS *Titanic* was launched on the 31 May 1911. At 46,328 tonnes, she was the largest passenger ship constructed at the time. She set sail on her maiden voyage on 10 April 1912 from Southampton, her route taking her to Cherbourg in France, then on to Queenstown (now Cobh) in Ireland. From there she left for New York carrying 2,223 passengers and crew.[1] At around 23.40 on the evening of 14 April *Titanic* struck an iceberg in mid-Atlantic. Despite being designed to withstand impacts of this kind by the construction of watertight compartments, the damage caused by the collision was too great. At 2.20

a.m. on Monday 15 April, the ship sank with the loss of over 1,500 lives.

As the quest for knowledge of the *Titanic* continues, attention has turned to the nature of the lost ship itself. Rediscovery through exploration of the wreck, and analysis of surviving documentation, photographs and personal accounts all confirm that she represented an extraordinary achievement born of supreme confidence. *Titanic's* designers and builders made full use of new technology and the industrial advancements of the age. The grandeur of the luxurious interiors and wide-ranging facilities, particularly in the First Class areas of the ship, has come to symbolize the opulence of the Edwardian period and of the years leading up to the First World War. They bear witness to a time of privilege and conspicuous consumption rarely seen before or after. The lavish interiors of First and Second Class contrast with the equally fascinating working areas of the ship, and the more spartan accommodation provided for the many Third Class passengers on board.

In many ways, *Titanic* was a product of established concepts of class and behaviour that were still rigidly adhered to. However, her time was one of major transition, when old traditions and new ideas coexisted, if not always comfortably. In fact, far from being a Golden Age of consistency and stability, the pre-First World War period was a time of technological, social and cultural upheaval as the old order sought to maintain the status quo in the face of rapid change. The horse and cart now shared the roads with the motor car; aeroplanes were venturing into the skies; and moving picture screens were being installed in music halls. Artists such as Matisse and Picasso were beginning to experiment with the depiction of abstract form, while Diaghilev's exotic and inspirational Ballets Russes took to the stage to delight and challenge audiences in equal measure. At the same time, there was significant social unrest, and ordinary working people in Britain and other Western states sought to improve their working conditions through strike action, bringing about shortages of coal and other commodities, which directly affected the smooth running of the great ocean liners.

The subject of the *Titanic* offers enormous scope for exploration of the people and history of her time, and their clothing, in all its many and varied manifestations, is a captivating aspect of a remarkable story. By examining what people wore, we gain a fuller and more rounded picture of what life was like on board. Clothing is of course just one component of the whole social picture, but it extends its reach into many other areas of the ship's history, and links the story of the *Titanic* to our own times. The very demographics of the ship's population offer a fascinating starting point: a comparatively small group of privileged and wealthy First Class passengers were billeted alongside, but strictly segregated from, much larger numbers of poorer travellers. The ship was a floating microcosm of 1912 society, still bound by the rigidity of a long-established class system and characterized by the polarisation of rich and poor, but experiencing the stirrings of change, both socially and culturally. The wide range of dress worn by those who sailed on *Titanic* offers not only an historic snapshot of fashion, but a springboard into the lives of virtually all classes and ages at a particular moment in time.

Titanic's facilities and interior decoration are important too, not just as the context in which garments were worn, but because the character and appearance of the ship had a direct bearing on the sartorial choices of its passengers. Opportunities for socializing in opulent and formal environments such as the First Class dining saloon called for appropriately smart dress, as dictated by social conventions and the current fashion. The range of sporting activities available required specific types of clothing, and the provision of large promenade areas, offering outdoor space in frequently windy and cold conditions, meant a need for warm yet fashionable outdoor dress. The sleeping quarters lead us to the more private activities associated with clothing, such as the process of dressing and undressing, and the many layers of underwear worn at the time.

The combination of old-world opulence and cutting-edge modernity embodied by *Titanic* was also reflected in the fashions of the era, in which the traditional and the novel existed side by side. During the period between 1908 and the outbreak of the First World War in 1914 there was a considerable style shift, particularly in women's fashions. In 1912 these were in the process of developing from the fitted and overtly feminine garments of the high Edwardian period, which owed much to the conventions of the late nineteenth century, to the eclectic and unrestrictive dress forms we associate with more modern times. In the new climate of artistic freedom and endeavour, forward-thinking designers like Paul Poiret were drawing inspiration from multiple sources in order to produce clothing that was both exotic and challenging. These innovations filtered down through the class layers of society, becoming diluted in the process, and by 1912 the fashionable silhouette had altered from the ultra-feminine hourglass figure to a much straighter line. However, the progression of fashion is never linear, and while these new developments went on around them, the older generation and those with limited money to spend stuck rigidly to the established Edwardian look. The convention of wearing layers of restrictive underwear also continued for most women, as did adherence to a strict set of rules for dressing for specific activities and particular times of day. Men's fashions, always slower to develop, were broadly similar to the styles prevalent in the 1890s.

A hundred years after she set sail, the fascinating and harrowing story of the *Titanic* continues to enthral. It is a story of grit and grandeur, triumph and tragedy. The wealthy passengers of First Class travelled in style, their many trunks and cases loaded with suits and gowns of the best quality and latest fashion, to be laid out for the day's many changes, and kept clean and fresh by a valet or lady's maid. When danger threatened, these people would be the first ushered into lifeboats, dressed in whatever they could grab. Further below decks, travellers of more modest means wore cheaper or second-hand garments, but were still dressed in their best for the voyage. Many of the poorest, travelling in large families with all their clothes and worldly possessions, were heading for a new life in America and a chance to escape from the system that kept them in Third Class. For too many, these dreams were about to be cut short, their clothes passing into history in the form of detailed descriptions made of their dead bodies when they were recovered. The same went for most of the crew, from the stokers and greasers dressed for the hard work of keeping the engines going; to the numerous stewards and waiters, who had to look impeccably smart but never showy; to the officers, dressed in uniforms that expressed the values of their profession: seamanship, diligence, courage and selflessness, all of which would be called for on the night of 14 April 1912.

2. Fashion and Status: Women in First Class

WHEN THE TITANIC weighed anchor and slipped out of Southampton docks on her maiden voyage, she carried 325 First Class passengers, drawn from the cream of British and American society. These included 145 women, many of them members of an élite class whose lives were shaped by conspicuous consumption, leisure and indulgence. Among their number were representatives from some of America's foremost families. Madeleine Astor, the new bride of Colonel John Jacob Astor—one of the wealthiest men in the world at the time—was sailing back to America with her husband after a prolonged honeymoon in Europe and Egypt. Eleanor Widener, the daughter of an American industrialist and leading light of Philadelphia society was also on board, while the most expensive suite on the vessel was taken by the much travelled American heiress Charlotte Drake Cardeza. British society was represented by, among others, Lucy, Countess of Rothes who was travelling to Canada, Mrs Julia Cavendish—an American heiress who had married into the English landed gentry, and Edith Pears, wife of Thomas Pears, whose family had founded the soap manufacturing company A. & F. Pears Ltd. Other First Class female passengers included the glamorous American model Dorothy Gibson, Margaret 'Molly' Brown, whose husband had made his fortune in the Gold Rush, the authoress Helen Churchill Candee and the fashion correspondent Edith L. Rosenbaum. The fashion world was also represented by the influential and highly successful couturier Lucile, known in private life as Lucy, Lady Duff Gordon.

While their backgrounds varied considerably, to a greater or lesser degree all the women of First Class would have conformed to the social conventions of the time, based on the rigid framework inherited from the Victorian era, which was only just beginning to break down. Clothing was an extremely important part of this, and to appreciate the sartorial rules and customs adhered to aboard *Titanic*, it is necessary to explore the wider context of fashions and dressing etiquette that shaped the lives of such women.

Fashion in this period was in a state of flux, and from around 1908 a metamorphosis was taking place. The ultra-feminine yet restrictive and cumbersome garments we associate with the high Edwardian era were disappearing, and in their place emerged a straighter line. It was a more liberated approach, which incorporated new and exotic influences, as well as imaginative techniques in both cutting and decoration. Ultimately these developments would lead to the revolutionary styles of the 1920s and beyond, but in the meantime, we find a rather mixed picture. Wealth did not necessarily mean that every woman in First Class slavishly followed new styles promoted by forward-thinking designers such as Paul Poiret. Instead, all but the most fashion-conscious opted for modified versions of more radical looks, and the older generation undoubtedly stuck to the more established styles associated with the Edwardian era which had just passed.

There is a wealth of information about fashions worn by female First Class passengers aboard *Titanic*, including photographs, personal accounts and magazines from the era. Perhaps the most revealing, for clothes actually worn by the passengers themselves, are some of the claims filed against the White Star Line after the sinking. These include a very detailed listing, running to eighteen pages, made by Charlotte Drake Cardeza, whose claim was the largest made by an individual.[2] It includes fourteen trunks, four bags, a jewel case and a packing case, containing property said to have been worth in total $177,352.75 (£36,567—equivalent to £2,084,319 today).[3] The majority of items are clothing, and the names of key fashion houses of the era such as Redfern, Rouff and Lucile, as well as the New York department store Lord & Taylor, are found throughout. Despite being a United States citizen, much of her wardrobe was purchased in Paris—the established high-fashion capital of the world.

Mrs Cardeza and her fellow passengers did not, however, receive the monies they sought. The final settlement between the White Star Line and all the claimants, approved by a U.S. court in July 1916, provided only $663,000 (£136,701) in compensation, with individuals receiving on average twenty percent of the sums asked for.

Lady Duff Gordon

Before exploring the many garments worn, we must note an extremely important player in the contemporary fashion world, who happened to be among the female First Class passengers. Lady Duff Gordon boarded the *Titanic* at Cherbourg, accompanied by her husband and secretary-cum-lady's maid. She was a fashion designer at the height of her success, with a newly opened branch of her couture house Lucile in Paris, a flagship establishment in London and a thriving offshoot in New York. Her clientele included some of the most fashionable women of the period, some of whom, such as Charlotte Drake Cardeza, and the Spanish newly wed Maria Josefa Peñasco, were numbered among her fellow passengers aboard *Titanic*.[4]

1 Portrait of Lady Duff Gordon wearing a Lucile gown (Bassano Studio, 1904).

Lady Duff Gordon's business was established during the 1890s when she was still known as Mrs Lucy Wallace; she married Sir Cosmo Duff Gordon in 1900. It was started out of necessity, since she had found herself in straitened circumstances after a failed first marriage. She chose the name 'Lucile'—a pet name she had had since childhood, and in a tough and competitive market she used her considerable talent for designing ultra-flattering feminine clothes to build a highly successful international business. She had a great flair for publicity, becoming an expert at generating exposure and making the most of every opportunity that arose. Lucile

2 Lucile evening gown, 1913, made from ivory-coloured silk charmeuse and chiffon, black silk velvet, and machine-made lace.

produced theatrical costumes for popular productions, which won her high-profile press coverage. At the same time she was dressing her society contacts, including her sister the famous novelist Elinor Glyn, in exquisite and highly desirable clothes, thus gaining an excellent reputation through word of mouth. Her rapid rise from home dressmaker to successful

couturier was therefore assured, and by 1909 she was at the helm of a thriving business.

The clothes themselves were renowned for being both flattering and alluring. Lucile claimed to be the first designer to make the woman her starting point, stating 'I always saw the woman, not the frock as detached from her.'[5] She felt it was important to dress women in clothes that flattered their individual figures and personalities, and she cited this as a key reason for her success. Edwardian women's clothing was extremely feminine, and in an era when soft pastel shades were the norm, along with a great array of trimmings, Lucile excelled at combining colour and ornament with skilful cutting to produce exceedingly attractive garments. She was adept at layering soft, semi-transparent fabrics embellished with glittering bead or sequin embroidery, which danced seductively in the light as the wearer moved. However, when the barometer of fashion changed she was at the forefront of new innovation, and steered seamlessly from the frothy, curvy lines of high Edwardian couture to the straighter, more sophisticated styles of the 1907–14 period, producing what was arguably some of her best work.

As well as creating an attractive, high quality product, Lucile set herself apart from other couture houses through a variety of new and different approaches to marketing. Her vibrant personality can be seen in the way that she chose to name her garments. She called them her 'Gowns of Emotion', and gave them titles such as 'When Passion's Thrall is O'er', 'Give Me Your Heart', 'The Sighing Sound of Lips Unsatisfied', and even 'Red Mouth of a Venomous Flower'.[6] These captured the imagination of fashion journalists and clients alike, as did her elaborate mannequin parades. Lucile claimed to have been one of the first to produce theatre-style productions in which beautiful hand-picked girls modelled her gowns for a select audience. Viewers were able to see the garments move on real bodies, rather than simply viewing them as drawings or mounted on static dress stands. Although today catwalk shows are an essential part of every designer's repertoire, for Lucile's clients they were a new and exciting way of understanding her clothes, making them an even more desirable prospect.

Lady Duff Gordon, along with her husband Sir Cosmo and her secretary Miss Francatelli, were making their way to the United States in order to oversee business matters relating to the New York branch of Lucile. In common with many of her fellow passengers, she was very impressed with the opulence and grandeur of 'this floating palace'. She occupied the First Class cabin A20, and recalled 'my pretty little cabin, with its electric heater and pink curtains, delighted me, so that it was a pleasure to go to bed'.[7] Except, of course, on the night of April 14.

A Glittering Social Event

For many of the First Class passengers aboard, sailing on the *Titanic* was much more than simply a means of getting from A to B. It was a social event, and tickets for First Class admitted the bearers to an exclusive five-day long party. Although often compared to the best hotels, the magnificent interiors of *Titanic*'s First Class were also designed to echo those of the great English country houses of the time. The scene, atmosphere and social context were set for the equivalent of a grand Edwardian house party, and women's clothing would have reflected this. We know about the complex dress codes adhered to on these occasions since towards the ends of their lives several well-connected women who belonged to pre-First World War society recorded them in their memoirs. Several refer to the strict rules governing clothing choices at this period, which might mean changing at least four times a day. Cynthia Asquith recalled:

> A large fraction of our time was spent in changing our clothes, particularly in winter when you came down to breakfast ready for church in your 'best dress' made probably of velvet if you could afford it, or velveteen if you couldn't. After church you went into tweeds. You always changed again before tea, into a 'tea-gown' if you possessed that special creation; the less affluent wore a summer day-frock. However small your dress allowance a different dinner dress for each night was considered necessary.[8]

Clothes were an essential part of the social whirl that wealthy women inhabited, and these established rhythms of dressing and undressing throughout the day were adhered to by the women of *Titanic's* First Class.

DRESSING FOR THE MORNING

Some First Class passengers took breakfast in their sumptuous Staterooms. Ordered in advance, it was brought by a room steward at the allotted time. This was the preferred choice for those who occupied the very best cabins, the 'Parlour Suites'. They were furnished to the highest standards, and the most expensive resembled luxurious city apartments, incorporating sitting rooms, opulent bathrooms and private promenades. In a letter written at the start of the voyage, Mrs Ida Straus stated: 'Our rooms are furnished in the best of taste and most luxuriously and they are really rooms not cabins'.[9]

A lady in First Class accommodation graced this grand and elegant environment with equally stylish clothing, carefully unpacked from a variety of bulky trunks and cases. To take breakfast in her rooms, she would probably have donned a peignoir over her nightgown. This was a luxurious full-length dressing gown of loose construction, normally with a generous collar, and fastened with ribbons fairly close to the throat, with further fastenings down the centre. During most of the nineteenth century the fabric tended to be plain, white cotton but by the end peignoirs had become more elaborate and colourful. During the high Edwardian era soft, floating chiffons in light pastel shades were favoured. Most incorporated decoration in the form of lace inserts, trimmings and ruffles, and some were constructed entirely of lace. The sleeves, often elbow-length, were usually wide, with generous flounces echoing those at the collar and hem. However, by 1912 the ultra-fashionable were opting for something more modern. Oriental influences were being seen

4 Bedroom of First Class suite B60 on *Titanic*.

in the newest fashions. Although these were much modified for day and evening wear, they remained less adulterated for items such as dressing gowns. The kimono style, essentially a T-shaped garment with floor-length skirts, was a natural choice. Usually made from lightweight silk, such dressing gowns could include elaborate and exotic embroidered decoration. In keeping with the very feminine nature of 'boudoir' clothing, lighter colours were still preferred, but the more radical adopted the new stronger reds or turquoise blues. First Class passengers such as actress and model Dorothy Gibson and socialite 'Molly' Brown numbered silk kimonos among the items lost in the sinking.[10]

Underwear

For those not breakfasting in their rooms, it was of course necessary to dress, often with the help of a maid: many First Class passengers brought a lady's maid with them. Although undergarments were beginning to be simplified by this date, dressing was still a time-consuming process, and assistance was required for the laying out and fastening of the many garments. For the younger set, the new narrower fashionable silhouette meant that the first layer was a light cotton or silk camisole, and directoire knickers—drawers that were much narrower and tighter in fit than previous forms, with elastic at the knees and the waist. They were closed drawers rather than those open at the crotch, which some women still continued to wear until around the First World War. As with all fashions, and particularly those for underwear, choices came down to personal preference and to some extent age. Many different forms of underwear were widely available, and the older generation continued the habit of wearing the lingerie styles of their youth. Chemises, some of which extended to just above the knee, were still favoured by some at this date. These were usually worn with the wide, open drawers—essentially two fabric tubes, gathered and stitched to the waistband, but with a gaping opening between the legs—a throwback to Victorian ideas of hygiene and convenience. For this style, the only concession to current fashions was the fabric: a light, soft material such as silk or fine cotton lawn, with lace inserts, rather than flannelette, thick cotton or wool, although these too were still available.

Another option for this layer of underclothes was a pair of combinations. These linked the chemise or camisole and drawers into an all-in-one garment, and had first appeared towards the end of the nineteenth century. Just like directoire knickers they too were a means of reducing bulk under closer-fitting clothing. Made with both closed and open drawers at this date, they were often prettily trimmed with lace, ribbons or white work embroidery. As with the peignoir, colour and lighter fabrics were now popular for undergarments. The 1870s and 1880s had seen women's underwear become increasingly decorative, colourful and luxurious. This trend continued through the twentieth century, and the house of Lucile was particularly known for its alluring and gossamer-fine lingerie, made of delicate coloured silks, still thought by some to be rather risqué.[11]

Over their chemise or combinations, most women donned a corset, which moulded the figure into the prevailing fashionable silhouette and dictated one's style of deportment. Paul Poiret and Lucile later asserted that they had successfully ousted corsets from the fashionable wardrobe, but in reality all but the most fashion-conscious and youthful continued to wear them for some years to come. It is certainly the case, however, that these new and influential fashion innovators had been responsible for a definite change in the shape of the corset. Poiret is usually credited with popularizing the straight silhouette and the corresponding high-waisted garments of his *directoire* cut, a line that precipitated a significant change in the construction of corsets from around 1908. Gone was the old Edwardian S-Bend style, with its tiny waist and straight front, which caused women to thrust their chests forward and the hips back in a stance which has been likened to that of a kangaroo. Instead corsets were now cut lower in the bust and extended much further over the hips, making sitting somewhat uncomfortable. They were still laced up at the back and clipped together at the front with stud and loop fastenings, but despite the familiar construction and heavy boning of steel or whalebone, the corseted waist was no longer pulled in tightly. This was a profound change in fashion which had not been seen since the high-waisted styles of the Regency period one hundred years earlier.

5 Pair of white cotton lawn combinations, with a silk tie at the waist and an open crotch, c.1890–1910. The neckline, legs, waist and armholes are trimmed with lace and cream satin bows.

With the lowering of the corset to a position below the bosom came a renewed need to support and shape the bust itself. Bust bodices had first made their appearance during the 1880s. They were constructed in a similar way to the camisole, but incorporated lines of boning. They had developed alongside bust improvers which, by the employment of adjustable sprung steels or tight frills of fabric, added the required dimensions to those not naturally endowed with a curvaceous figure. By 1912 the full, rounded

The Spécialité Corset Regd.

THE CORSET IS NO LONGER AN INSTRUMENT OF COMPRESSION,

and although it must not be apparent that one is worn, it is a more important factor in woman's dress than ever before.

The dresses of to-day require a Corset in which the lines and graceful willowy motions of the figure have no restraint.

This effect is obtained in the models of the "Spécialité" illustrated, which give the wearers that expression of natural grace and freedom of motion without any sacrifice to comfort, allowing the muscles above and below the waist to act independently of each other.

The prices of the "Spécialité" are no more than you pay for **Good** Corsets elsewhere; but in addition to their incomparable cut and shape is the fact that they are boned with **Real Whalebone,** which means they retain their original shape until worn out and in the end constitutes them the **Cheapest Stay on the Market.**

TYPE 27.   TYPE 25.

THE "SPÉCIALITÉ" CORSET.

TYPE 27 (as illustration).—This new model for 1912 is in "Maillot Suède," a delightfully soft material. It is only slightly boned, and most suitable for evening wear or when only the slightest support is required. In pretty shades of Pale Blue, Pink, White, and Grey... **31/6**

THE "SPÉCIALITÉ" CORSET.

TYPE 25 (as illustration).—This, the latest model, is cut very low above the waist-line to allow of an extreme décolleté, and extends in sweeping unbroken lines well down on the hips. Sixteen firm real Whalebones, cleverly distributed, give sufficient support to improve and hold the slight or medium figure in a perfectly firm and reliable manner, but it must not be considered a suitable type for stout figures. Price with three pairs of suspenders **21/-**

DICKINS & JONES LTD., REGENT STREET, LONDON, W.

bust of the fashionable 1890s and early 1900s was no longer in vogue, marking the decline of the bust improver. However, bust bodices increased greatly in popularity and, according to the Oxford English Dictionary, 1912 was the year that the word 'brassière' was used for the first time in Britain, and references to the word have been found as early as 1907 in American women's magazines.[12]

However, broader influences than those of high couture were at work in the development of undergarments at this time. New-style short corsets, which definitely required separate bust support in the form of a brassière, were being developed in response to the craze for the Tango. This energetic and passionate dance was taking the world by storm at the time of the *Titanic*. Shorter corsets and supported busts were vital to attempt its athletic and jerky movements, and those who had experienced the greater freedoms that these garments provided inevitably began to adopt them for everyday use. Women's supportive underwear was thus moving much closer to the pieces we are familiar with today, and the brassière was well on its way to becoming a wardrobe essential.

Whether long or short, the bottom edge of the corset usually incorporated suspenders. They were of solid, heavy construction, and clipped to stockings at a point just above the knee. By this date the best stockings were made from knitted silk and came in a variety of soft, pastel shades, although for day wear during the colder months wool stockings were worn. The petticoat completed the undergarments which, although still complicated to modern taste, had become considerably simpler and more streamlined compared to what had been worn less than a decade before. In keeping with the fashion for new slender skirts, the petticoat too had changed from the gathered, flounced Edwardian version into a narrow tube of silk or fine cotton, of which only one was worn, rather than the multiple layers required to support the wider skirts.

6 (opposite) Advertisement for the 'Spécialité Corset' by Dickins and Jones, *The Queen, The Lady's Newspaper*, March 1912. It illustrates how manufacturers were acknowledging that corsets were now required to shape the body in a more natural and discreet way.

This could be fastened at the waist in the traditional way, often with a matching camisole above to prevent the corset showing through the outer layers. Alternatively, a full-length version, which incorporated the camisole, might be selected. This was the Princess petticoat, or the slip, as it was now known. With the donning of the petticoat, the foundations were at last complete for the outerwear to follow.

The Tailor-Made Suit

During the morning, in keeping with the sartorial rules of the period, women passengers dressed in practical garments designed for comfortable travel and active leisure pursuits. Although the weather on the voyage was said to have been fairly settled, it was only April, and the ship was heading towards the colder climate of the Northern Atlantic. With this in mind, the sensible choice of clothing for morning was the tailor-made suit. Usually made from face-cloth, worsted wool, or tweed, and originally evolving from sports clothing, the tailor-made had first emerged during the 1880s, and was popularized by fashion leaders of the day such as Princess Alexandra. The best examples were extremely alluring. They were faultlessly tailored by firms such as Redfern and Creed, fitting the wearer like a glove.

The suit continued to form part of many women's wardrobes through the 1890s, and gained even greater popularity during the Edwardian era. The practical nature of the tailor-made was now associated with more liberated roles for women within society, and with the rise of the Suffragette movement. The fashion persisted into the time of the *Titanic*, and in no garment of the time was the new, straight silhouette more evident. For the most fashion conscious it included a hobble skirt, said to have been introduced by Paul Poiret who famously stated, 'Yes I freed the bust, but I shackled the legs'.[13] Skirts tapered down to a very narrow opening at the ankles, making it almost impossible to walk. In reality, very few women actually followed this fashion slavishly: the tailor-made was far too practical a garment to be compromised in such a way. As Mary Howarth of *Everywoman's Encyclopaedia* stated, 'it is very awkward not to be able to get into trains and cars without forcible assistance, and...there are many ways of making the skirt look straight and tight and at the same time

8 (overleaf) Advertisement for tailor-mades by Peter Robinson's of Regent Street, *The Queen, The Lady's Newspaper*, March 1912.

9 (overleaf) Hand-coloured fashion plate featuring outdoor wear from the supplement to *Supplement au Vrai Chic et au Guide des Couturières Réunis* magazine, July 1910. It shows the new narrower silhouette and includes high collars as well as a low, softly-ruffled one.

4905

N° 13 1er Juillet 1910

C. Reymond Directeur Gérant

Imp Valloton & Crespin Paris

Reproduction interdite

SUPPLÉMENT AU VRAI CHIC

ET AU

GUIDE DES COUTURIÈRES RÉUNIS

ABEL GOUBAUD, Fondateur

ADMINISTRATION :

3, Rue du 4-Septembre, PARIS

10 Gooch's advertisement for a hip-length jacket and skirt. It features simple button and braid decoration and is worn with dainty shoes and spats. *The Queen, The Lady's Newspaper*, March 1912.

At GOOCH'S LIMITED EST 1835

Brompton Rd. London. S.W.

COURT DRESSMAKERS

ADVANCE SPRING MODELS

Charming
COAT AND SKIRT
for young Ladies' wear,
in Navy, cream, and coloured
coating serge.
Coat lined satin.
Price 57/6
We specialise in small sizes.

WRITE FOR NEW ART CATALOGUE.

of securing width.'[14] Flat pleats or slits were incorporated towards the hemline, thus allowing the skirt to retain its fashionable narrow shape without hampering the legs. The hem level also rose to just above the ankles to aid walking. On the top half of the body a jacket was worn, over a white cotton or silk blouse, the latter often trimmed with frills at the neck and chest.

Crisp white blouses with lots of details in the form of tucks and ruffles were extremely popular during the Edwardian period, and continued afterwards in simpler modified form. High collars, wired to keep them upright, were ubiquitous during the early part of the twentieth century and some passengers were certainly still wearing them. Lady Duff Gordon, claimed to have abolished the high boned collar, although she was not the only designer to have developed new styles. She stated: 'No woman who has not worn one can possibly imagine how horrible it was to have one's throat scarred by sharp collar supports made of either whalebone or steel, which ran into one with every movement, so that the head had to be kept rigidly in a most unnatural position'.[15] She advocated more open necked designs such as the Quaker Girl collar and the Peter Pan neck which were at first criticized for being unhealthy, but soon became part of the general fashionable look.

By now the jacket had moved away from the ultra-fitted styles of the previous decades. It tended to be long and loose in the waist, and extended to well below the hips. It was usually asymmetrical in cut, and might feature contrasting colours at the collar (which often included broad lapels), pocket flaps and cuffs, as well as oversized buttons. Decoration was kept to a minimum. In winter, simple fur trimmings were also acceptable. Popular colours were muted browns, greys, or navy. Suitable for sport, country outings, morning wear in town, and particularly travel, this classic garment was both practical and stylish and, in modified form, has remained a wardrobe staple right up to the present day. Elegant leather boots, sometimes of two contrasting colours, were worn with a suit, or shoes with laces. For the more practical, heels were usually low to facilitate walking, and often of the Louis shape, but narrow high-heeled shoes were also worn outside by the fashion conscious, even in the winter months, sometimes with protective spats. Others opted for black patent leather shoes with a square buckle at the front.

Thus attired for breakfast and the morning's amusements, the First Class lady passenger was now ready to make her way to the *Titanic*'s public areas. Breakfast was taken in the First Class dining saloon, which extended across the full width of the ship, and was spacious and extremely grand. The decoration included an elaborate moulded plaster ceiling, while slender pillars and archways broke up the space. Like all the meals available to First Class passengers, breakfasts were lavish. Lady Duff Gordon recollected feeling 'childishly pleased on finding strawberries on my breakfast table. Fancy strawberries in April, and in mid-ocean. The whole thing is positively uncanny...Why, you would think you were at the Ritz'.[16]

Promenading

If the weather were fair, the morning's routine would almost certainly include a walk along *Titanic*'s First Class promenade. This activity was undertaken as much for being seen as for taking the air, especially on this particular voyage, which numbered so many fashionable and wealthy people

11 Two passengers take the air on *Titanic*'s First Class promenade.

among its passengers. Promenading was an established pastime for all classes of passenger, and *Titanic*'s designers had ensured that all the open decks could be used for this pursuit. The principal First Class promenade area was on A Deck. Deck-chairs were to be found along much of the promenade, and these could be booked ahead to ensure a good position from which to enjoy the view, both of the sea and of the other passengers. For those who wished to be more active, games such as shuffleboard and quoits were often played on deck, and nets for tennis and cricket were also available.

Since promenading was an important social activity, the women of First Class ensured that they were dressed stylishly in outdoor wear appropriate to the weather. To accompany their smart and beautifully cut tailor-made suits they required several important accessories. Gloves were worn, not just for the practical purpose of keeping the hands warm, but as also as an essential part of dress, whatever the weather. Most First Class passengers followed traditional rules of etiquette, which required women to wear gloves whenever they were in public, excepting main meal times. The rules regarding the wearing of gloves had been established during the nineteenth century, and were gradually being eroded by this date, but for the most part established norms continued, with only the most daring breaking free. Traditional concepts of propriety still dictated that physical contact, except in the most private situations, was inappropriate. Gloves therefore provided a barrier during social interaction for which contact was unavoidable, such as shaking hands.

For everyday wear gloves were elbow-length, made of leather or suede, often with sixteen buttons running up the inside of the arm from the wrist. In order to emphasize the slender nature of the hands, they were cut extremely tight, and could take up to twenty minutes to put on. For extra warmth,

12 Three wide women's hats, c.1909–12, lavishly trimmed with ostrich feathers, imitation flowers and velvet.

13 Pair of long black suede gloves, lined with white kid leather, c.1900–14.

One of the smartest Hats of the season. Can be produced in most of the leading shades 7½ gns.

To describe in their full splendour and magnificence the new Hats for the season is a task beyond the power of words A visit is cordially invited.

Derry&Toms
KENSINGTON HIGH STREET. W

14 Advertisement for a striking ostrich feather trimmed hat from Derry and Toms department store, Kensington High Street, London. *The Queen, The Lady's Newspaper*, March 1912.

expensively fur-lined gloves were also available and might well have been worn aboard *Titanic*. Muted colours such as browns or greys were popular for gloves, and many pairs were required, as they quickly became dirty, and might be changed several times through the day. After the sinking, First Class survivor Dorothy Gibson claimed for dozens of pairs of gloves, both long and short, from the White Star Line.[17] The very highest quality gloves were made to measure, although ready-made versions were also available, with the best coming from France. In her book *The Cult of Chiffon*, Mrs Pritchard states that 'a really well-dressed woman has her gloves made for her with as great care as her boots, although nowadays we can get the best makes and be almost perfectly fitted.'[18] Shops such as L.T. Piver served a wealthy clientele, and had branches in both London and Paris, selling only the finest French ready-made gloves.

Social etiquette during this period also dictated the almost universal wearing of hats. The era of the enormous and lavishly trimmed picture hats had reached its pinnacle around 1910, and by 1912 they had begun to shrink, but were still highly elaborate and of considerable size, with decoration becoming more vertical in nature. Small and practical felt hats were worn with some tailor-made suits, but it was still common to see women wearing large, elaborate hats even with the simplest clothing. The craze is said to have begun around 1907. As skirts narrowed, hats broadened, and by 1910 and 1911 the correct proportions were said to be three to two: the circumference of the hat being six feet and the skirt hem four feet.[19] They were often called Merry Widow hats, in reference to one worn by Lily Elsie in the 1907 London production of Léhar's operetta of the same name. Lady Duff Gordon was associated with this trend too: she had designed her costume, and the wide straw hat, trimmed with ostrich feathers, which went with it. It is said to have sparked a fashion still current at the time of the *Titanic*. Ostrich feathers were always a favourite trimming, but other plumage was also used, such as that of aigrettes or birds of paradise. These feather trimmings, which decimated the exotic bird population, were derided by the Society for the Protection of Birds, which lobbied parliament for a ban, but little success was achieved against the forces of fashion until after the First World War, when the style had fallen from favour. For day wear, particularly in cooler weather, generous silk and velvet hat trimmings were common, usually in dark or muted colours.

These enormous structures required support, and a feature of the high Edwardian period was a cult for wide hairstyles, extending out in puffs on either side of the face. They bridged the gap between the head and the hat, and for those not endowed with thick, wavy hair, false hair (sometimes called 'rats'), pads and frames were used to add volume. By 1912 hairstyles had begun to shrink in line with the reduced size of head wear, but false hair was still used, as were hatpins. These were often highly decorative, with their length reflecting the size of the hats and hairstyles that they had to penetrate.

The ostentatious fashion for large hats did not go unnoticed by satirists and social commentators. Being so

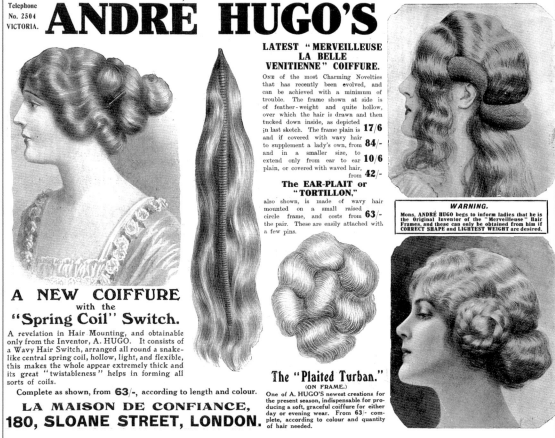

ANDRÉ HUGO'S

A NEW COIFFURE
with the
"Spring Coil" Switch.

A revelation in Hair Mounting, and obtainable only from the Inventor, A. HUGO. It consists of a Wavy Hair Switch, arranged all round a snake-like central spring coil, hollow, light, and flexible, this makes the whole appear extremely thick and its great "twistableness" helps in forming all sorts of coils.

Complete as shown, from **63/-**, according to length and colour.

LA MAISON DE CONFIANCE,
180, SLOANE STREET, LONDON.

LATEST "MERVEILLEUSE LA BELLE VENITIENNE" COIFFURE.

ONE of the most Charming Novelties that has recently been evolved, and can be achieved with a minimum of trouble. The frame shown at side is of feather-weight and quite hollow, over which the hair is drawn and then tucked down inside, as depicted in last sketch. The frame plain is **17/6** and if covered with wavy hair to supplement a lady's own, from **84/-** and in a smaller size, to extend only from ear to ear **10/6** plain, or covered with waved hair, from **42/-**

The EAR-PLAIT or "TORTILLON,"

also shown, is made of wavy hair mounted on a small raised circle frame, and costs from **63/-** the pair. These are easily attached with a few pins.

WARNING.

Mons. ANDRÉ HUGO begs to inform ladies that he is the Original Inventor of the "Merveilleuse" Hair Frames, and these can only be obtained from him if CORRECT SHAPE and LIGHTEST WEIGHT are desired.

The "Plaited Turban."
(ON FRAME.)

One of A. HUGO'S newest creations for the present season, indispensable for producing a soft, graceful coiffure for either day or evening wear. From 63/- complete, according to colour and quantity of hair needed.

15 Advertisement for hair pieces, *The Queen, The Lady's Newspaper*, March 1912.

conspicuous, they were much criticized, especially in anti-suffrage circles. The impractical nature of female fashionable dress was used as ammunition against female claims to political rights, and hats were a particular target. In his 1912 book *The House of Commons from Within*, Robert Farquarson sought to undermine women through commentary on their clothing choices. He stated that they 'possess a selfish and cynical indifference to the convenience and safety of others, as is shown by the preposterous erection they proudly bear on the top of their heads'.[20]

Further items of clothing were needed to be both warm and fashionable when promenading on deck. An alternative

URBITOR
BURBERRY.

WEATHERPROOF Topcoat for either wet or dry weather, combining the services of both garments with distinctive Burberry advantages of its own.

AIRYLIGHT, the acme of comfort for walking, driving, or motoring.

SAFEGUARDS against cold winds and draughts, preserving healthful temperature in all weathers.

EXCLUDES wet by Burberry Weave and Proof.

BECOMING and Smart, in artistic colourings and original patterns, THE URBITOR fulfils every town or country need both of ornament and utility.

PATTERNS, PRICES, AND ILLUSTRATED BROCHURES SENT POST FREE ON REQUEST.

NOTICE.

BURBERRYS have added extensively to their proofing works for the purpose of carrying out a new cleaning process whereby fresh life is given to a practically discarded Burberry Coat.

THE URBITOR BURBERRY.

BURBERRYS Haymarket LONDON
8 and 10, Boulevard Malesherbes, PARIS
Basingstoke; also Agents in Chief Provincial Towns

16 Advertisement for an Urbitor Burberry topcoat, which was both weatherproof and lightweight, *The Queen, The Lady's Newspaper*, March 1912.

to the tweed jacket was the short, knitted sports coat, which fell to just below hip level. It was loose and often belted, and resembled a thick cardigan in style. It had started out as golfing attire, but from around 1909 it began to be worn more generally as part of informal clothing. If the weather was wet, a Burberry gabardine coat might be worn. The firm had patented this twill woven fabric, the yarn for which was treated to make it waterproof, during the 1880s. It was used in the production of both men's and women's garments during the 1900s, including motoring coats and overcoats. The fabric gained enormous popularity after it was worn by polar explorer Roald Amundsen, the first man to reach the South Pole, in 1911. Ernest Shackleton also wore it when he led his expedition across Antarctica (1914–17).

As *Titanic* headed north, a full-length winter coat would have been essential against the chilly winds of the Atlantic. Many overcoats were made from thick wool, designed as either double or single breasted, and colours ranged from pale camel through to black. Although some were tailored to fit, most did not follow the figure too closely, thus providing room for the more streamlined clothing beneath. Some coats had fur trimmings, but for the most opulent effect, full or three quarter length fur coats were also worn. In her autobiography *The Rainbow Comes and Goes*, Lady Diana Cooper mentions being given a full-length coat of ermine by a suitor during this period.[21] Fur was extremely fashionable, and a Harrods catalogue from the time stated, 'Furs again dominate. In every form the pelt is favoured. It adorns the hat and evening frock with equal success, and the gracefully modelled coat and set is a *sine qua non* with the well dressed'.[22] Sable was perhaps the most fashionable, but the choice was extremely broad. In her insurance claim against the White Star Line, Charlotte Drake Cardeza listed a variety of furs including seal, ermine, chinchilla, silver fox, mink and white baby lamb.[23] The Harrods catalogue mentions a coat and set, and the set refers to the fur accessories worn over the coat. These generally consisted of a generous stole, which was draped over the shoulders, and an oversized muff, usually held quite high up and away from the body. The entire pelt of the animal was used in such accessories, including the heads and tails. The overall effect was one of extreme wealth and luxury, as fur was of course very expensive. The aforementioned Harrods catalogue priced a sable set at 108 guineas.

Leisure Pursuits

Titanic's female First Class passengers had a wide array of indoor activities at their disposal. Many of them were designed to encourage social interaction in the most luxurious and, for a ship, sometimes novel, surroundings. For the more active, a gymnasium, Turkish baths and a swimming bath supplemented the traditional deck-based sports. Much of the gymnasium equipment was primarily intended for men, but some was specifically designed for female passengers. The writer and *Titanic* survivor Helen Churchill Candee recalled testing the exercise equipment in the gym during the day before the sinking, and activities aimed at women included the horse riding machines and bicycle racing. Two cycling machines were fixed side-by-side, allowing passengers to race each other against the clock. Women would not have owned clothing specifically for wear in a gym at this date, although they did actively participate in outdoor sports such as tennis, golf and riding, all of which had their own particular forms of dress.

For cycling, which had been an extremely popular female pursuit since the late nineteenth century, knickerbockers or divided skirts could be worn, but by 1912 improvements in bicycle design meant that many women simply wore a loose skirt and blouse. Certainly one of the 'electric horses'

17 The First Class gymnasium on *Titanic*.

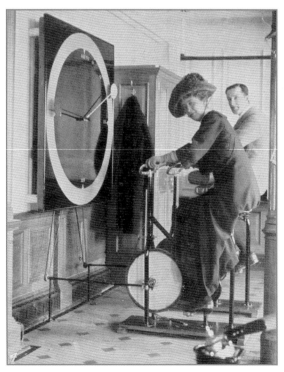

18 Mr Lawrence Beesley and a friend try out the cycling machines in the gymnasium. They are not wearing suitable clothing, as they were simply exploring the ship's facilities when the photograph was taken.

was built for female passengers, since it was designed to be ridden side-saddle, still the way that most women of the British upper classes rode horses, although some more daring American women and their younger British counterparts were riding astride in divided skirts or modified jodhpurs. Women's riding habits were made to measure by a tailor, and the top half resembled a man's suit with a fitted jacket and waistcoat. They were made from very fine wool in dark colours, and the skirt was specially cut so that it retained a regular length all around as the wearer sat on a horse—a style known as the apron skirt.[24]

The *Titanic*'s First Class facilities included Turkish baths, which were exotically decorated with painted tiles on the walls and had luxurious reclining seats. Given the prevailing attitudes of the time, the concept of women using the Turkish baths seems slightly surprising, since it required the removal of much of one's clothing in a semi-public area. However, for certain periods during the day the baths were

20 First Class Café Parisien on *Titanic*'s B deck.

reserved exclusively for women, and at this time only female attendants were present. Evidence that women used and enjoyed Turkish baths is to be found in Lady Diana Cooper's memoirs. She was a keen swimmer, and recalls 'after an hour's tuition my friends and I, wrapped in bath-towels, would stagger into the hottest room of the "Turkish," send for large strawberry ices from Gunter's next door and shock the older, fatter ladies with our giggling gossip'.[25]

Swimming too was available on-board ship. Along with its sister ship *Olympic*, *Titanic* was one of the first liners to have a swimming pool. It was situated alongside the Turkish baths on F Deck, and, as suggested by the quote above, it was envisaged that the two facilities would be used in tandem. The sides of the deep tank were much higher than the water level to prevent the water overflowing when the boat

21 The First Class reading and writing room on *Olympic*.

moved. One entered the pool room, decorated throughout with blue and white tiles, via a marble staircase. A row of dressing cubicles was situated alongside the pool, and here female passengers changed into their bathing clothes. Some still wore shorter, more streamlined versions of the belted serge tunics favoured by the Victorians. These extended to just above the knee and were worn with matching bloomers, but from 1910 the one-piece bathing suit had come into more general wear. It was still made from either serge or jersey, and hung loose and heavy when wet.

If First Class passengers wished to enjoy a drink or snack in the middle of the morning, they had at their disposal the Café Parisien as well as the cafés in the twin Verandah and Palm courts. The Café Parisien was located on B Deck. It served meals and light refreshments between 8 a.m. and

11 p.m., and passengers sat in wicker chairs around elegant wooden tables. The decoration attempted to bring the outdoors indoors, in imitation of a French pavement café: a light and airy space with large windows. Wooden trellis panelling was affixed to the walls and ceiling, some of it with imitation climbing plants. The café quickly became a popular meeting area, and First Class passenger Henry Julian remarked that 'The Parisien café is quite a novelty and looks very real...it will no doubt become popular amongst rich Americans.'[26]

Those who wished to read could borrow books from the First Class library, and there was also a First Class reading and writing room with silk-upholstered chairs, elegantly draped curtains and potted palms. The decoration was feminine in style, and, although not strictly segregated, the area was intended as a quiet retreat for female passengers, equivalent to the smoking room that was reserved for men. For light and gentle indoor pursuits, chess, draughts, cards and dominoes could be borrowed from the library steward. Other areas for relaxation and socializing included the First Class lounge, an elegant space designed in the Louis XV style, in imitation of Versailles, with oak panelling, large windows and a beautiful marble fireplace.

LUNCHEON

Before lunch, passengers assembled in the reception rooms of the ship's two main restaurants, the dining saloon and the à la carte restaurant, where music was provided by a quintet and a string trio respectively. Lunch itself was a formal affair served by a myriad of waiting staff. It consisted of a minimum of three courses and could last for up to two hours.

For lunch, women were expected to change out of their functional tailor-mades, as a more formal atmosphere reigned in both restaurants. Fashionable formal day wear also followed the new straight silhouette, with the waistline reasonably high, in the Empire style. The new open necklines, which were often V-shaped, and sometimes softly draped in the cross-over style, usually featured semi-transparent modesty in-fills or were worn with a separate upper chest covering called a chemisette. Sleeves were often elbow-length, but flesh was not supposed to be fully visible at any time other than when a woman was actually eating, so gauze or chiffon under-sleeves, extending to the wrists, and almost skin-tight, were sometimes incorporated into garments. If under-sleeves were not part of the ensemble, then elbow-length gloves would fill in the gap. Gloves for smart indoor wear were usually of white kid leather rather than of the darker shades worn outdoors. As with the tailor-made, skirts generally followed a narrow line, with some

(phot. Reutlinger.)

Raudnitz
(phot. Manuel.)

4898

Nº 12. 16 Juin 1910

C. Reymond Directeur-Gérant.

24 Corsage watch of gold and green guilloche enamel with a central pearl on the back. The face is edged with pearls and the watch is suspended from a bow-shaped gold and enamel brooch. Late 19th to early 20th century.

being cut in the 'hobble' style. Others were made more comfortable through pleating and carefully positioned slits towards the hem. Skirt decoration, either in the form of trimmings, or of layered and asymmetrical draping, was beginning to come to the fore at this time, with draped, pleated or artfully trimmed tunics or overskirts breaking up the straight silhouette at knee level or below. Skirts often featured a small train, even for day wear, and lighter-weight stockings in muted colours were worn, some with simple decoration in the form of clocks at the ankle.

Fashionable colours were bolder than the soft pastels favoured until around 1908. Blues, rich dark reds, greens and purples were all popular during the winter and spring of 1911 to 1912, and fabrics were fairly substantial, with velvet a popular choice. Embroidered decoration, especially appliqué and beadwork, was not confined to evening wear, but was frequently to be found on smart day dress. Jewellery was worn during the day, but in a restrained form. A simple oval brooch might be pinned at the throat or a bar brooch positioned elsewhere on the bodice. A long string of beads was also popular. Timepieces were also now being worn

23 (opposite) Designs for fashionable day wear from the *Supplement au Messager des Modes*, June 1910, showing the new long, slender silhouette, high-waisted style and the use of tunics to break up the line of the trained skirts.

by women. Wristwatches were available, as were highly decorative enamelled and jewelled corsage watches. To complement this smarter indoor outfit, lighter-weight shoes were worn. At this time they tended to be fabric-covered, have Louis heels, and a high tongue. Hats were obligatory— toned to complement the rest of the ensemble, probably of a smaller circumference than those worn for promenading. These newly fashionable smaller felt hats were round or oval in shape, with simple upturned brims and upstanding aigrette or osprey feather trimmings.

AFTERNOON

After lunch passengers retired to their cabins, or relaxed in the various and lavishly decorated public areas of First Class. More active pursuits, particularly outdoor-based, necessitated a further change of attire into more practical clothing along the lines of that discussed for the morning's activities.

The late afternoon was traditionally a time of relaxation, and at five o'clock afternoon tea was taken. This was available in the various cafés located around the First Class areas and was also served in the First Class lounge. If taking tea in the ship's public areas, female passengers would have remained in their semi-formal day wear. However, those whose staterooms incorporated separate reception rooms took tea amongst a more select coterie in the privacy of their suites. Here they donned tea-gowns to receive their guests. Although they had existed as part of the female wardrobe since the late 1870s, the tea-gown is particularly associated with the leisured decadence of the Edwardian era. They were diaphanous, loose garments, designed to be worn without corsets. As such they offered a certain level of relief from the constricted nature of

25 (opposite) This black tea-gown, made from fine silk crepe and lace, dates from the mid to late 1890s. Although features such as the puffed sleeves are typical of the 1890s, tea-gowns of the Edwardian era were similarly loose and flowing in appearance. Outwardly such a gown appears to be a very relaxed garment, but underneath a tightly boned bodice shapes the figure much as a corset would.

female clothing, and marked the transition between the day's activities and the formality of evening wear, allowing the wearer to relax and the body to breathe. Liberty gowns, as produced by the famous London department store, were frequently worn as tea-gowns during this period. Inspired by mediaeval garments, and hinting at the artistic sensibilities of the wearer, they were originally intended as 'aesthetic dress' and worn only by those who were against the prevailing corseted form. However, by 1909 they had crossed over into mainstream fashion as the ideal garment for afternoon relaxation.

DRESSING FOR DINNER

Dinner aboard *Titanic* must have been a particular highlight for First Class passengers. It was designed to provide all the luxury and theatre of the finest city restaurants, which in turn imitated the traditions and opulence of the great houses of the day. The importance and formality of the occasion was established from the very start, and the ship's bugler played the tune of 'The Roast Beef of Olde England' to summon passengers to dinner. Once seated, the First Class dining saloon offered a different ten-course menu every, night featuring the finest fresh produce, skilfully prepared by an army of cooks. Passengers enjoyed the typically rich dishes of the day, and the menu from the night of April 14—the last dinner on the *Titanic*—lists courses of oysters, soup, salmon with mousseline sauce, sauté chicken Lyonnaise, a choice of roast beef, duckling or lamb, roast squab, punch, cold asparagus, paté de foie gras, and, among various puddings, Waldorf pudding, French ice cream or chocolate and vanilla éclairs.[27] The dinner service was of fine bone china edged with designs in 22 carat gold, the cutlery was silver plated, and the glassware cut crystal.

Diners in the à la carte restaurant paid extra to enjoy an even wider and more varied menu in exceptionally lavish surroundings. The restaurant was designed in the Louis XVI style, featuring light walnut panelling with elaborately carved and gilded ornaments. Reeded and gilded pillars stretched up to an elegantly moulded ceiling, and rich, deep pile carpet covered the floor. The restaurant had been a huge success on *Titanic*'s sister ship *Olympic*, and on *Titanic* it was extended to provide room for fifty tables, although intimacy and selectivity was maintained by keeping many of them for two diners only.[28] Edward J. Smith, Captain of the *Titanic*, attended a dinner there on the night of the sinking. It was hosted by the wealthy and influential Widener family, and the guest list included several of the leading social figures aboard. Guests would have enjoyed drinks in the adjoining reception room to the strains of the ship's string trio before heading into the restaurant to begin their lengthy gourmet dining experience.

For the women of First Class, such a lavish and formal dining ritual required a suitably luxurious evening wardrobe. Many ensured that their extensive luggage included a different outfit for each night, and First Class staterooms and suites were furnished to provide space for the large number of different ensembles required. Some of the best suites had adjoining wardrobe rooms, and all First Class cabins had at least one mirrored wardrobe. As with the morning's toilette, assistance from a maid or female room steward was often needed for the lengthy task of undressing, dressing and preparing one's appearance for the evening ahead. Every layer of clothing was changed, to complement to best effect the more delicate and revealing garments worn for the evening.

After replacing a plain cotton chemise with a silk version, a sturdy, functional day wear corset might be

Artist's impression (1911) of the First Class elevator on *Olympic*.

swapped for a more elegant and decorative model selected in a fabric and colour that toned with the garments to be worn above. The best corsets now came in a wide variety of colours, and were finished with high quality fabrics such as silk satin. Others were embellished with decorative embroidery. Wool or cotton stockings were changed for silk ones, and these were available in different colours to complement particular garments. Those with flamboyant tastes could opt for stockings with lavish, embroidered or sequined designs such as coiling snakes. Silk petticoats were necessary for the smooth fitting of evening dress. The new fashionable slim line required streamlined petticoats made from crêpe de chine or Japanese silk rather than the rustling paper taffeta or glacé silk versions favoured during the earlier years of the twentieth century, and probably still worn by the older generation.

At some point during the dressing process a female passenger would sit down at her mirrored dressing table. In

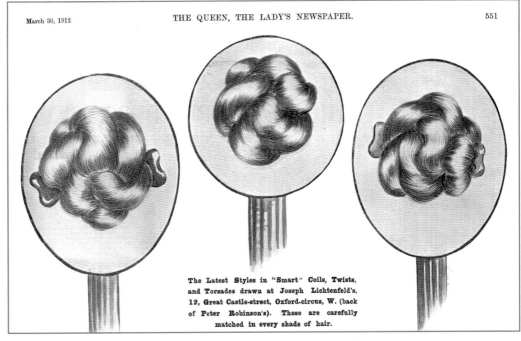

The Latest Styles in "Smart" Coils, Twists, and Torsades drawn at Joseph Lichtenfeld's, 12, Great Castle-street, Oxford-circus, W. (back of Peter Robinson's). These are carefully matched in every shade of hair.

most of the standard First Class staterooms this was made from mahogany, with a matching chair. Whilst the subject was seated, her hair was arranged in one of the elaborate styles of the day, by her maid if she had one. Those without maids arranged their hair themselves or called upon the services of the ship's hairdresser. The new styles had less width and height than those of a few years earlier. Hair was parted either at the side or in the middle, smoothed over the top of the head and then given more volume by curling and pinning into place at the back and sides. The most fashionable opted for 'Marcel waves', which sat snugly against the head, a hair fashion that was to become ubiquitous during the 1920s and 1930s. To aid the production of the perfect coiffure, electric curling tongs were fitted in every First Class cabin.

Although officially still frowned upon in polite society, the use of cosmetics was becoming more widespread during this era. Cosmetics advertisements appeared in women's

27 Examples of hairstyles from 1912, note the newly fashionable Marcel waves as well as the elaborated coiled coiffures. *The Queen, The Lady's Newspaper*, March 1912.

L.1754

magazines, but they tended to emphasize the discreet nature of the products they recommended. A natural, healthy complexion was favoured, and make up was normally limited to the use of light powders to overcome shine, whilst tinted lip salves and rouge were judiciously applied by the more daring. Scent too was worn. The Edwardian period had seen the use of light, floral perfumes with names such as 'May Blossom' or 'Moss Rose', but the new, more exotic fashions led to the creation of scents with spicier, headier notes such as 'Phul-Nana', an extract of Indian flowers.[29] Paul Poiret produced a successful perfume range in 1911, and was the first of many fashion designers to do so.

Evening wear during this period exuded glamour and sophistication. The newest styles seemed impossibly exotic and daring. Although his clothes were worn only by the ultra-fashionable and artistic set, it is important to mention the work of Mariano Fortuny. He was inspired by Ancient Greek sculpture, and his famous Delphos gowns were radically modern and incredibly glamorous. Stunning, tightly pleated silk dresses edged with Venetian glass beads fell in an uninterrupted line from shoulder to hem, utilizing only discreet drawstrings to adjust fit at the neck and arms. However, perhaps the most important designer experimenting with a new slender silhouette and stronger colours was Paul Poiret. His style was at its most striking in the evening wear he produced. Poiret had opened his own Paris fashion house in 1904, and from around 1907 started to produce high-waisted Empire Line dresses. As his designs evolved over the next few years, they drew inspiration from many different sources, including Middle and Far Eastern dress and European regional costume. He swathed the body in beautiful draperies, and made use of sumptuous fabrics in strong colours, with exotic decorative devices. Society's increasing acceptance of the new mode was due in part to the success of Serge Diaghilev's Ballets Russes. The lavish

28 (opposite) Design for an elegant and diaphanous high-waisted evening gown from the *Supplement au Messager des Modes*, February 1910, showing the fashionable cross-over bodice, elegantly draped sleeves and overskirt.

sets and costumes designed by Léon Bakst for productions such as *Schéhérazade* captured the public imagination and caused a craze for all things oriental.

The most fashionable First Class female passengers are therefore likely to have donned an elegant Poiret-inspired evening gown (if not a model created by the great man himself). As mentioned above, the waistline was cut higher than the natural level, giving a straight, slender silhouette. Bodices were sometimes draped in the cross-over style, featuring fairly low, wide necklines, and short, loosely cut sleeves. However, contemporary concepts of social propriety meant that for dinner the revealing nature of these styles was sometimes toned down by the inclusion of semi-transparent silk chiffon or tulle. Narrow skirts clung suggestively to the legs, often featuring a small train at the back. By 1912 the line of the simple, slender skirt had become increasingly complicated by overskirts, artful draperies, or tunics, which added decorative detail and broke up the skirt line at around knee level. Many variations were achieved, and the style offered imaginative designers the opportunity to add a wide selection of decorative devices such as lace, embroidery, bows and fabric flowers. Opulent fur trimmings, stitched around hems, necklines and cuffs, were said to be particularly attractive in combination with chiffon for evening wear.[30]

Silk in the form of satin, chiffon, gauze, velvet or brocade was the favoured fabric for evening, and the new strong, bold colours included rich, deep reds, blues and greens as well as gold and turquoise. However, as with all fashions, not every woman adhered to the prevailing trends, and a good proportion opted instead for colours that suited their complexions or time of life. Despite embracing the new fashionable line, Lucile, Lady Duff Gordon's couture house, prided itself in dressing clients in clothing that took account of their figures and skin tones, sometimes flying in the face of the fashionable palette. In her memoirs Lady Duff Gordon

29 (opposite) A 1912 evening ensemble comprising a 'lampshade' skirt and tunic entitled 'Sorbet' by the highly sought-after fashion designer Paul Poiret. It is made from silk chiffon and satin, embroidered with glass beads and trimmed with fur.

30 (overleaf) This lavishly embroidered cream satin evening gown by the talented designer Madame Clapham dates to around 1902 and is typical of high Edwardian fashions. The older generation continued to opt for evening wear which was closer to this in cut and style.

wrote: 'I think that many designers of the younger school are far too inclined to turn out their models "en masse", regardless of the special needs of women who will wear them, and so they lack personality and interest.'[31] Her establishment was known for favouring gentler, pastel shades in soft, pliable fabrics and she gives the following description of a dress of 'soft grey chiffon veiling an under-dress of shot pink and violet taffeta. It looked rather like an opal, and gave the impression of something shadowed and unreal.'[32] Surface decoration was very important in evening wear, with glittering beadwork embroidery being a particularly popular choice. Often worked upon semi-transparent fabric that draped beautifully from the weight of the glass beads, it glinted in the low and intimate light of the dinner table. The many hours it took to produce such decoration added to the expensive and luxurious effect. Those who chose to dress in less up-to-date styles would have selected aspects of modern dress that suited their more conservative tastes. The glamour of a scattering of beadwork decoration might still have featured, but the dresses themselves had natural waistlines and wider skirts.

In keeping with the opulent nature of its women's clothing, this era was known for the lavish flaunting of expensive jewellery. Passengers were advised to take valuables to the Purser's office to be locked away, but items could be retrieved for a smart dinner, and less important pieces were kept in cabins so that they could be worn during the course of the voyage. Eleanor Widener had reportedly been advised by insurers Lloyds of London to keep her multi-strand pearl necklace (valued at £150,000 or $750,000 at the time) within her sight during the entire journey.[33] Stories of priceless jewels owned and lost by First Class passengers abound. Eloise Hughes Smith, a honeymooning 18-year-old, had wanted to retrieve jewellery from her room before climbing into a lifeboat, but her husband prevented her from doing so, thus probably saving her life, although he himself

31 This striking evening coat is attributed to Paul Poiret. Made from black silk satin with a green shot silk lining, it features a chemical lace collar and bold multi-coloured embroidery with a Middle Eastern flavour.

died in the sinking.[34] Violet Jessop, a room steward who subsequently wrote her memoirs, recalled passing empty First Class cabins as the ship was sinking: 'How strange it was to pass all those rooms lit up so brilliantly, their doors open and contents lying around in disorder. Jewels sparkled on dressing tables and a pair of silver slippers were lying just where they had been kicked off.'[35]

Several female survivors made claims against the White Star Line for jewellery they had lost. Nineteen-year-old Helen Walton Bishop claimed to have lost property worth about $20,000. The jewellery consisted of a platinum chain with a diamond plaque, a pearl necklace with an emerald drop, sixteen rings set with diamonds, sapphires and emeralds, a string of pearls, a string of corals and two or three pairs of emerald and pearl earrings.[36] Charlotte Drake Cardeza's jewellery included items from the prestigious firm Tiffany & Co.: a Burma ruby and diamond ring worth $14,000 and a pink 7-carat diamond valued at $20,000.[37] Diamonds were particularly favoured during the high Edwardian period, and were by this date perhaps more likely to have been worn in quantity by the older generation. Long strings of pearls or jet beads were also seen with the new fashions, some with the addition of a choker. The Art Nouveau style was still influencing jewellery design, but the prevailing fashion for classical modes meant a new craze for jewellery inspired by ancient Greek and Roman art, and large cameos and plaques, embellished with diamonds and pearls, were popular. Long, drop earrings complemented the hairstyles of the day, and jewelled hair ornaments, sometimes incorporating feathers, were also worn. Lavish and boldly styled bracelets and rings with dark or colourful stones adorned wrists and fingers.

Before leaving her cabin, the lady First Class passenger would have slipped on silk-covered shoes to co-ordinate with her outfit. Evening shoes of this period had elegant Louis-style heels, almond-shaped toes, high tongues and sometimes jewelled buckles. It was also necessary to add extra warmth with an evening coat or wrap, since the weather became increasingly cold during the course of the voyage. This period produced some stunning examples of outerwear for evening, since the prevailing fashion for drapery and opulence lent itself to the lavish styling of such garments. Poiret was particularly known for his evening coats; cut in the style of Japanese kimonos and swathing the wearer in silks and rich gold brocades, they featured bold decoration such as large tassels, heavy fringing and embroidery inspired by middle and far eastern decorative art. Fur was also an obvious choice for evening wraps and coats.

AFTER DINNER

As several accounts of people's last hours aboard *Titanic* survive, it is possible to build up a picture of the sorts of evening pursuits followed after dinner. Some returned to the restaurant's reception room to take coffee and to hear the ship's orchestra play. Others played card games in the First Class lounge, or repaired to the Café Parisien for hot toddies. Those with large parlour suites invited fellow passengers to their rooms for further conversation and drinks. Then, socializing over, it was time to undress for the final time that day, don one's nightgown and slide into bed. Lavish wooden bedsteads with lace covers graced many First Class rooms, while the very best suites featured four-posters. The nightgowns of this era were long, loose garments, made variously from silk, cotton or fine wool, depending on the level of warmth required. The neckline tended to be V-shaped in keeping with daytime bodices, and if a waist seam was present, it was high. Lace trimmings were used in abundance, especially around the neck and cuffs, and other decorative devices such as ribbon bows and vertical tucks were also common. Pretty boudoir caps, with lace and ribbon decoration, were worn by some.

Thus ended another day of elegant and elaborate dressing for the privileged women of *Titanic*'s First Class. Little did these individuals know that on the night of April 14 they would be woken and asked to rush to lifeboats, grabbing what clothes they could for warmth and leaving much of their finery behind on the sinking ship. Lady Duff Gordon recalled how once aboard a lifeboat she had teased her secretary Miss Francatelli about the strange mixture of clothes she had flung on in such a hurry, saying, 'just fancy, you actually left your beautiful nightdress behind you!'[38] As well as other layers, Lady Duff Gordon herself is said to have worn a lavender kimono-style dressing gown, a blue head wrap and a coat of squirrel fur.

When disaster struck, the Duff Gordons and Miss Francatelli were all able to board Lifeboat One. In the general confusion just twelve of its forty places were filled, and the Duff Gordons were questioned as part of the subsequent enquiry. Due to the 'women and children first' rule, many of the male passengers had perished after failing to secure places on lifeboats, so some of those that did survive were later labelled as cowards. Sir Cosmo had also caused controversy since he had offered cheques to the sailors aboard his lifeboat, which could have been interpreted as bribery. He was vilified in the press and is said never to have recovered from the scandal. Lady Duff Gordon and a fellow survivor, the fashion correspondent Edith L. Rosenbaum, discussed their mutual interest in fashion aboard their rescue ship *Carpathia*, commenting that 'pannier skirts and Robespierre collars were at a discount in mid-ocean when you are looking for a ship to rescue you.'[39]

3. Dressed for Display: Children in First Class

IN CONTRAST TO MODERN passenger ships, *Titanic* had no areas or facilities specifically devoted to children. In part, this was in line with prevailing views, which, although much more liberal than one hundred years earlier, still required children to fit in with, and cause minimal disruption to, the adult world. Contemporary sources reveal that upper class attitudes towards children could be very distant, and even neglectful by modern standards, although there were always exceptions to the rule. In her memoirs Cynthia Asquith recalls that at grand country house parties the hour after tea was children's hour, when 'down they stumped in their sashes and necklaces of amber or coral beads, to be entertained with Peep-Bo, Ring-a-ring-a-roses'.[40] Otherwise they were not seen. In fact, only seven families travelling First Class brought young children with them: the Carters, the Dodges, the Odells, the Lenox-Conynhams, the Speddens, the Ryersons and the Allisons. The last three brought their nannies, leaving the parents to relax and enjoy the ship's facilities. Seven children, aged from eleven months to thirteen years old, stayed on board for the Transatlantic crossing, the others were spared the horror of the disaster because their families were only travelling as far as Cherbourg or Queenstown.

32 One of the twin Verandah and Palm Courts on board *Olympic*.

Children would have been present in many of *Titanic's* public areas during the day, getting to know one another and creating play opportunities where they could. On *Titanic's* sister ship, the *Olympic*, the starboard Verandah and Palm court had become a gathering place for smaller children and their carers. Identical facilities aboard *Titanic* were probably adopted for similar purposes.[41] Deck-based games such as quoits and shuffleboard also doubtless became a focus for older children. As to their clothing, children were no longer dressed in barely modified replicas of adult garments, and did now have their own fashions, albeit still cumbersome by comparison with modern equivalents.

UNDERCLOTHING

Towards the end of the nineteenth century, dress reformers had successfully influenced the modification of children's dress, and the boned corset was no longer a part of children's wear. However, Victorian attitudes towards the importance of warm and often restrictive underwear were still prevalent in 1912. Babies were particularly well wrapped up in many layers, and layettes of the period include large numbers of underwear items. As well as quantities of cotton lawn shirts, the Army and Navy catalogue for 1907 recommends the purchase of swathes, in both linen and wool flannel. A swathe was a type of binder, designed to be wrapped around the infant's body very like a swaddling band. Some babies may even have been tied into stiffened or quilted staybands at this time. Pilches of flannel were also listed. These were squares of material secured over nappies for warmth and protection.[42] Dr Jaeger, whose Sanitary Woollen System had first become popular during the 1880s, was still very influential in early twentieth-century households, and many parents adhered to his recommendation that babies wear wool shirts next to the skin, even the softest of which probably caused itching and discomfort.

This conscientious wrapping up of the young was not restricted to babies. Children too were dressed in layers of underclothing that today seem excessive. Except in warm weather, when linen or cotton versions replaced them, both boys and girls wore wool chemises or vests with separate cotton or wool flannel drawers. Although plainer in style, the cut was similar to those worn by adults, and drawers were open or closed at the crotch according to preference. An alternative, which also echoed adult underwear styles, was a pair of combinations, first popularized by Dr Jaeger. These were usually made from woollen jersey, and were frequently worn by children at this time. A well-known brand for children's underwear during this period was Chilprufe, which was launched around 1911, and is still in production today. The name sought to reassure parents about the protective qualities of the product, indicating that the Victorian fear of chills had not diminished.

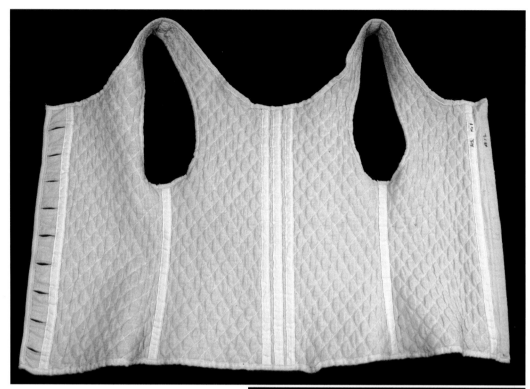

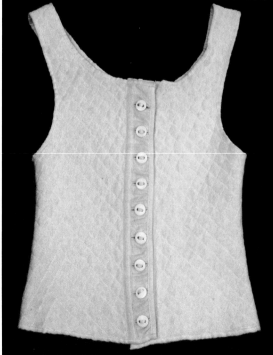

33 An original Liberty Bodice from 1908. It is made from unbleached knitted cotton, with strapping at the back and sides, and fastened with bone buttons. There are more buttons around the waist to attach button-hole drawers. Suspenders could be attached by the two side straps.

Several manufacturers of children's underwear, including Chilprufe, were also making reinforced and quilted bodices for both boys and girls, designed to be worn over a vest or combinations. These had their roots in the late nineteenth-century stay bands or binders (which in their turn had replaced boned corsets for children). As well as providing warmth, they also had a supportive role to play, since it was still generally believed that children's growing bodies required external control in order to grow effectively without deformity. The most famous of these garments was the Liberty Bodice, which was launched by R. & W. H. Symington of Market Harborough in 1908. It was intended to be more comfortable than corded and stiffened binders, yet provided gentle support for growth and, of course, protection from the dreaded chills. It was a simple sleeveless garment made from knitted cotton stockinette with button fastenings at the centre. Cloth straps were stitched down the back and sides to provide some rigidity, and buttons were added at waist level and below for the attachment of drawers and stockings. At the height of its success Symington was producing over three million liberty bodices a year and they remained in production until 1974.[43]

After donning a bodice and buttoning drawers in place, girls then rolled on wool stockings—usually of black wool and held up by elasticized garters, although some girl's bodices incorporated suspenders. Boys wore long woollen socks, which completed their underwear. For girls, a cotton or flannel petticoat was added to their ensemble. Petticoats resembled those worn by women of the period, except that they were shorter, finishing just below the knee. White was the usual colour for girl's underwear of the period, but, just as in women's fashions, pastel colours were beginning to appear, while red flannel petticoats were still worn by some.

Babies were not confined to cabins or other indoor spaces whilst aboard *Titanic*: nannies would have taken full advantage of the access to fresh air that the generous First Class promenade decks supplied. Babies' rigid daily routine at this time included lengthy walks outdoors in a pram, regardless of cold weather. As Nanny McCallum recorded of her training with the Tate family (of Tate and Lyle sugar): 'After potting, there were clothes to wash and mend. Then out for a walk. And we did walk—from eleven-thirty till lunch'.[44] Large gatherings of uniformed nannies pushing roomy Landau–style perambulators were a common sight in London's parks during this period, and perhaps the three nannies who travelled on *Titanic* met in the public and open-air spaces on board in much the same way.

The emphasis on fresh air meant that babies were often on show in public, so they were dressed in clothes that were both warm and highly decorative. The outward appearance of babies and children was generally deemed to reflect the social standing and wealth of a family. So status, as well as fashion and hygiene, determined the choice of colour for babies' clothes. White was almost universally worn, and the ability to keep such clothing spotlessly clean at all times signified a family's ability to employ enough staff to wash, mend and press the many items required. A continuation from the Victorian era was the use of long robes, although they were not as long as they had been before prams were introduced in the mid nineteenth century. Such robes were heavily trimmed with whitework embroidery, lace, tucks and flounces, and often incorporated features such as puffed sleeves and generous collars. Caps, too, were seen as essential for warmth and decorative effect. Babies' caps and bonnets were even more elaborate than their robes, since they framed the baby's face and were highly visible when

seen in a perambulator. For warmer weather, these were made from white cotton and trimmed around the face with several frills of lace or whitework. Knitted or crocheted caps of soft, fine wool were fashionable for colder days.

Outerwear included woollen jackets, pelisses (long jackets of cotton fastened with buttons or drawstrings), and long capes or cloaks of wool—usually cashmere for its softness. These might be lined with quilted silk, and decorated with further white embroidery or applied silk braid. The feet were

34 Miss Freda Gray as an infant, wearing elaborate white garments including a lavishly trimmed cap, c.1900–15.

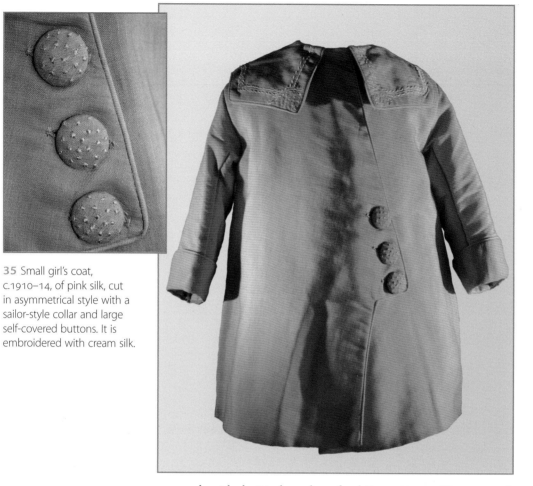

35 Small girl's coat, c.1910–14, of pink silk, cut in asymmetrical style with a sailor-style collar and large self-covered buttons. It is embroidered with cream silk.

covered with knitted socks of white cotton, silk or wool, over which soft kid leather or wool shoes were worn, held in place by a bar across the top of the foot and fastened with a tiny button. In addition to these many layers, a baby might also be tightly wrapped in a knitted woollen shawl for warmth and to prevent excessive movement.

Toddlers' clothing, like that of babies, was often very elaborate, cumbersome, and difficult to care for. The only concessions were that long robes were shortened to mid calf length to allow movement, and darker colours might be seen, as well as more robust fabrics such as cotton

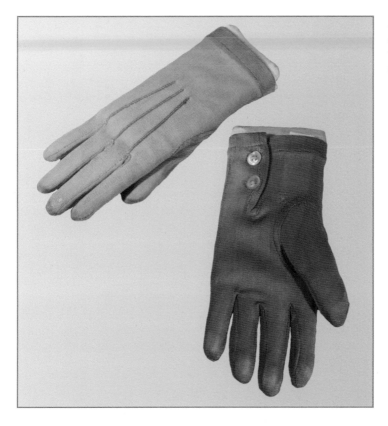

36 A pair of girl's silk knitted gloves, c.1900–14. Openings at the wrist are fastened with two mother-of-pearl buttons.

37 Child's tan leather button boots with leather soles and gold thread tassels. Early twentieth century. They are marked with 'Size 2, Classic Customgrade'.

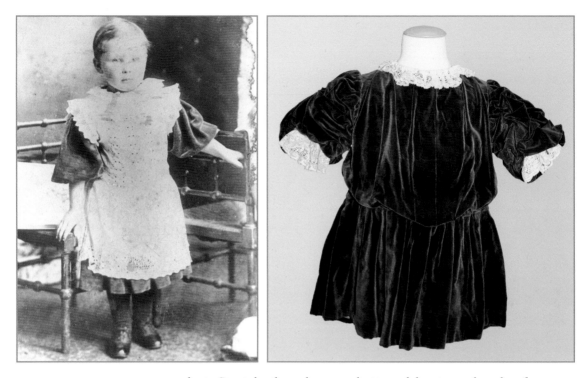

velvet. Stout leather shoes or buttoned boots replaced soft woollen footwear for outdoors. At first glance it is often difficult to distinguish girls from boys in pre-First World War photographs. This is because the long tradition of clothing boys in dresses until the age of four or even later still continued. Close inspection reveals less elaborate, yet still frequently long hairstyles for boys, in addition to slightly less fussy decoration on clothing. But both clothing and appearance were essentially unisex.

OUTERWEAR FOR OLDER CHILDREN

Afforded slightly less supervision than their younger siblings, the older children of First Class are likely to have been encouraged to form friendships as they played in the public areas of the ship—their parents safe in the knowledge that the strict segregation of passengers into different classes prevented any undesirable acquaintances from being formed. Favourite toys and activities were stowed in hand luggage, ready for use during the voyage, and store catalogues of the period are full of imaginative and exciting items for children. For example, the 1914 Gamages catalogue includes elaborate model cars and trains as well as 'harmless pistols and cannons'.[45] The child educationalist Friedrich Froebel, whose ideas had found particular favour from the 1870s onwards, recommended that children should be encouraged to do creative tasks: drawing, painting and the study of nature, and kits for craft-based activities such as making threadwork pictures and beadwork baskets were widely available. These would have been ideal for keeping children occupied during the voyage, while simple games such as rolling hoops along the endless decks would also have been popular. The excitement felt by adults at being on board such a new and massive ship must have been magnified tenfold for children, who revelled in the chance to explore such a remarkable vessel.

Miss Lucile Polk Carter and her brother Master William Thornton Carter II, thirteen and eleven years old respectively, and Master Denis Lenox-Conyngham and his sister Eileen, who were ten and eleven, were among those who had that unique opportunity.[46] Eileen Lenox-Conyngham wrote to her nanny, Louisa Sterling, during the first leg of the voyage, and her words evoke some of the wonder felt by the children who travelled on *Titanic*: 'Dear Luisa, The *Titanic* is the biggest ship on the world there is a swimming bath a gymnation Turkish baths in it'. Later in life she recalled her feelings as she explored the boat:

> We were absolutely staggered at how enormous the *Titanic* was because we'd been used to the small cross channel boats, and her size and the beauty of her lines she was absolutely lovely! Unbelievably lovely!! I just remember the

sight of her when we came on board. Just the enormous size and the beauty of the lines and then we were able to go all over the ship...and we had I remember a lovely luncheon in the dining room with its arched staircase and things...It was so lovely, all the fittings were so lovely...the glass and the china and the flowers, everything was brand new.[47]

It was not until after the First World War that garments began to be designed to appeal directly to the tastes of children, but some concessions to practicalities and ease of movement had crept in during the second half of the nineteenth century, and these had fully taken hold by the time of the *Titanic*. These changes were partly due to a growing acknowledgment of the importance of childhood and children's rights, but dress had also been specifically targeted by reform groups. Since the 1880s groups such as the Rational Dress Society had been actively campaigning against tight lacing and the unhealthy nature of fashionable clothing. They had little success in reforming adult clothes, but made significant strides in improving children's wear. The emergence of a separate group of garments designed specifically for children was also due to the success of the Aesthetic Movement, which emphasized the need for artistic and natural clothing.

Sailor Suits

One type of child's garment that reflected the ethos of these reforms, although its introduction actually preceded them, was the sailor suit. This attractive yet practical ensemble had first found favour during the 1840s when the young Prince of Wales wore one aboard the royal yacht, and it continued to be very popular well into the early twentieth century, when it was adopted by both boys and girls. It consisted of sturdy white or navy cotton trousers or shorts, or a skirt for girls, a loose sailor blouse with a navy collar

39 Boy's sailor suit, c.1910–20, of white cotton twill with separate navy cotton collar and cuffs. The cap is embroidered in gold with 'HMS *Tiger*'.

attached, a knotted neckerchief and a hat. This could be a straw sailor hat, a round cloth sailor cap (complete with ship's name), a peaked cap or a straw boater. Sailor suits were popular with parents and children alike. For parents they were a simple, smart, uncontroversial and patriotic choice. Children favoured them because they appealed to their sense of fun and enjoyment of fancy dress. Katharine Moore mentions how she longed for a sailor suit when she was a girl: 'I would wear a Holland smock or a pink, blue or

40 Advertisement for 'Charming Tunic Suits for your Little Boys' by Samuel Brothers. The suits are inspired by historical dress in the mode of the Little Lord Fauntleroy suit. *The Queen, The Lady's Newspaper*, March 1912.

white stained cotton frock, but never, oh never my heart's desire—a sailor suit, navy and white with a whistle in the side pocket and a round sailor's cap with HMS *Victory* or *Britannia* on the ribbon in gold'.[48]

Sailor suits were worn by all social classes, and child passengers aboard *Titanic*'s First and Second Class would undoubtedly have had at least one sailor suit in their luggage, their enthusiasm to wear it perhaps all the greater for actually being on board ship.

Boy's Clothing

Another outfit still worn by boys during this period in both Britain and America, and perhaps worn for smart lunches in the First Class dining saloon of the *Titanic*, was the Fauntleroy suit. First popular during the 1880s, it was usually reserved for best dress. Just like the sailor suit, it was a form of fancy dress that had migrated into mainstream wear, but its adoption was clearly associated with the romantic preferences of mothers rather than the independent choices of their sons, who tended to become the butt of other boys' jokes when wearing one. The suit consisted of shorts, with a jacket of black velvet with a wide lace collar, and was often combined with long curled hairstyles and shoes with large buckles. The style was based on early seventeenth-century dress, and was popularized by Frances Hodgson Burnett's novel *Little Lord Fauntleroy* in which the main character wears such a suit. Compton Mackenzie perhaps voices the opinions of many boys of the time when he recalls:

> ...that confounded Little Lord Fauntleroy craze which led to my being given as a party dress the Little Lord Fauntleroy costume of black velvet and Vandyke collar...Other boys... were inclined to giggle at my black velvet, and after protesting in vain against being made to wear it I decided to make it unwearable by flinging myself down in the gutter.[49]

Once they were too old for Fauntleroy suits, boys were often dressed for best in Eton suits. These were based on the uniforms worn at Eton College, but became a much more widespread fashion both in Britain and abroad. The suit consisted of a short black wool jacket with wide lapels worn open over a waistcoat, and matching or lighter coloured trousers. A wide, stiffly starched white collar was folded down and overlapped the jacket collar, and was sometimes finished with a bow tie at the neck. A top hat was the usual head wear worn with the Eton suit.

For everyday wear the comfortable and practical Norfolk jacket might be worn, with either knickerbockers or shorts to match. This was also an adult fashion, but whereas men usually wore them only for outdoor sporting pursuits, boys wore them far more frequently. The jacket was made from tweed, or plain dark blue or black wool, and featured two box pleated sections, which ran from shoulder to hip. The jacket also had a belt of the same material, which buttoned into place at the front. Originally designed for sports such as shooting or golf, the Norfolk jacket had ease of movement incorporated into its design, and was seen as a suitable garment for active young boys before they graduated into replicas of adult lounge suits and Chesterfield overcoats in their mid teens.

A new alternative to the Norfolk suit was the Buster Brown suit, which had emerged around 1908. This was the first of many fashions to cross over from America to Britain, and was based on a popular American comic strip character.

The suit featured wide bloomer-style trousers that finished at the knee, and a double-breasted hip-length jacket cut with a rounded neckline. A wide starched collar, similar to the Eton collar, was worn with it, along with a black silk bow at the throat. A round straw hat completed the outfit.

Just like men, boys were expected to wear hats at all times when out of doors. Where not dictated by the requirements of specific ensembles, these tended to be flat, peaked caps. Footwear also varied according to different outfits, but practical, laced leather boots were frequently worn, or sturdy leather lace-up shoes. For less formal wear, and for warmth, children at this time often wore a knitted pull-over, a popular version of which was the Guernsey, stitched 'in the round', often with decorative patterns. Boy's jerseys with 'stand-up collars in navy blue' were available to order from the Army and Navy catalogue, and were no doubt particularly suitable for chilly sea breezes.

Girl's Clothing

With the exception of the sailor suit, girl's clothing generally followed the line of adult female fashions until late into the nineteenth century. Even into the Edwardian period, 'best' clothing remained restrictive and cumbersome, although more everyday garments reflected new attitudes towards children, and allowed for more freedom.

For smart occasions, younger girls wore heavily starched white cotton dresses, trimmed with elaborate embroidery and lace flounces. Coats of cotton piqué or wool, featuring further trimmings, were worn over these, along with kid leather or silk gloves, and oversized bonnets, tied with large silk bows and embellished with extensive trimmings, just like those of their mothers. For best, older girls might wear their skirts fairly long, with short jackets featuring puffed sleeves, long boots with many buttons, long woollen coats

4900 E

and bonnets. These garments were not designed for activity, but rather for the sensible, quiet behaviour associated with formal occasions or Sundays, when boisterous games were not encouraged. They restricted movement, and were prone to becoming damaged and dirty very easily. In fact, they were in themselves a means of controlling girls' behaviour. The importance of keeping the Sabbath as a quiet, reflective and religious day was adhered to throughout much of Western Christian society, and for children the lack of play opportunities, coupled with restrictive clothing, was a particular trial. Mary Keen recalled:

> There was just a feeling in the air. You daren't laugh and all your toys and books had to be put away...I had one special frock for Sunday and a top petticoat. In those days, I was bundled up from the top down to my boots. This petticoat had a starched top which used to cut into my neck. It was so painful that when it got to tea time, I would look at the clock, thinking, 'God, only another two hours before I go to bed'. I was so glad to take that thing off.[50]

The Sabbath was fully observed aboard *Titanic*, with divine service conducted in the First Class dining saloon. Passengers of all ages would have been expected to follow quieter activities and to wear smarter clothing.

Everyday wear was a little more forgiving than Sunday best, and younger girls wore quite plain frocks of wool, cotton or silk, according to the weather. At this period these had full skirts cut just below the knee. The typical style featured a yoke or smocking at the chest, from which the fabric fell freely without a waist seam, and incorporated wide sleeves gathered in at the cuff. The smock style was derived from the clothing of rural farm workers and adopted as a comfortable, simple form of dress for young girls. Colours might be light pastel shades, although darker colours were often favoured in the winter months. This fashion had first emerged during the late nineteenth century, and was

42 (opposite) Fashions for girls of varying ages, *Supplement au Vrai Chic et au Guide des Couturières Réunis*, July 1910. The dropped waistline, which was to make its way into women's clothing during the 1920s, is clearly in evidence here.

linked to the principles of the Aesthetic Movement. Girls' education also included a new emphasis on gymnastics and outdoor games, and school uniforms consisted of unfitted, comfortable serge gym tunics that hung loosely from the shoulders without constriction at the waist. These too had an influence on mainstream fashion for girls.

Pinafores were another key aspect of girls' clothing at this time. Made from starched white cotton that was kept spotlessly clean, they were worn from the top to the bottom of society. Ostensibly designed to protect the dress beneath from being soiled, the pinafores worn by wealthier girls had by this date taken on a decorative rather than protective role, with elaborate frills, flounces, embroidery and pin tucks. Although sleeveless, they usually had generous frills at the shoulders, or incorporated yokes with frills all around. Pinafores followed the line of the dress and did not have a waist seam. They were made with generous amounts of material, pleated to provide fullness, and they fastened at shoulder blade level with a sash or buttons, hanging loose and open below.

The Tailor-made suit so frequently worn by women during this era was also found in modified form in the wardrobes of older girls. A Harrods advertisement in *The Queen* of March 1912 shows several different styles. All resemble the adult versions in their trimming, asymmetrical cut and hip-length jackets, but they are much less fitted, with loose, just-below-knee length skirts to allow for ease of movement. The Daphne is described as an 'elegant coat and skirt in fine face cloth and best cheviot serge. Coat panel back finished [with] hand braided ornaments to correspond with the front...suitable for young ladies 10 to 16 years'.[51] They are recommended as ideal for wear at school, but they would have been equally suitable for travel, especially during cooler weather. Similar versions were doubtless worn, with wide brimmed hats and leather gloves, on the decks of the *Titanic*.

The advertisement reads:

Harrods

are now showing some exceptionally attractive

School Outfits

including smart and serviceable

DRESSES, COSTUMES, and BLOUSES ——

for Misses of all ages.

An opportune moment to acquire everything that a young Lady needs in replenishing her wardrobe for Easter and the forthcoming Term.

Harrods direct special attention to their new models in Tailor-made SUITS, all of which are cut and completed on the premises by competent men tailors.

J.C. "DAPHNE." Elegant Coat and Skirt in fine face cloth and best cheviot serge. Coat panel back finished hand braided ornaments to correspond with front. Stocked in all the newest colourings. Suitable for young ladies 10 to 16 years.
Price, first size 59 6 rising 4 -.

J.C. "GLADYS." Useful Coat and Skirt in creme cord coating and navy and creme serge. In sizes for young ladies 10 to 16 years.
Price, creme cord first size 45 - rising 4 -.
Price, serge first size 35 - rising 3 -.

J.C. "GWENDOLEN." Misses' Coat and Skirt in a variety of light Tweeds finished with a contrasting face cloth. Coat panel back and lined polonaise, also similar style in navy serge.
Price, 52 6.

J.C. "BEATRICE." Misses' Coat and Skirt in a fine cord suiting. Coat lined shot silk, collar buttons and buttonholes finished with soft contrasting colours. Stocked in navy, black, creme, and a variety of colours.
Price, 4½ gns.

J.C. "ENID." Spring Coat and Skirt in Cheviot serge Panel back, in dainty shades of blue, reseda, and rose. Stocked in sizes to fit young ladies 10 to 16 years.
Price, first size 32 6 rising 2 6

HARRODS L^TD RICHARD BURBIDGE Managing Director LONDON · S · W

DAPHNE   GLADYS   GWENDOLEN   BEATRICE   ENID

CARRIAGE PAID on all Drapery purchases within the United Kingdom.

Orders by Post receive individual attention, and are executed with the utmost dispatch.

Perhaps children leaving the ship at Cherbourg, like the Lenox-Conynghams, envied those who remained on board, expecting to enjoy *Titanic*'s splendours all the way to New York. Of the latter, the Carter children and both their parents got safely away in lifeboats, as did the Speddens and their nanny. The Ryerson children and their mother got away too, although only after their nanny had objected to 13-year-old Jack being treated as a man and expected to stay behind with his father, who was to perish. The Allison family did not fare so well. Their nanny got promptly into a lifeboat with her charge, baby Trevor, but Mrs Allison, unaware of this, refused to leave without him or her husband, and got out of her own lifeboat to go and

43 Harrods advertisement for girl's tailor-made suits or 'costumes', here recommended as school outfits. *The Queen, The Lady's Newspaper*, March 1912

find them, taking her daughter Loraine with her. Eleven-month-old Trevor was thus the only member of the family to survive, thanks to the decisive action of his nanny, and, perhaps, to his very warm clothes.

4. Of Conservative Cut: Gentlemen in First Class

ENJOYING TITANIC'S First Class accommodation on its historic voyage were some extremely wealthy and influential men. One of the most notable was Colonel John Jacob Astor IV, the 47-year-old multi-millionaire, who owned a huge New York property portfolio. He was returning to New York with his pregnant new wife, Madeleine Astor. Another famous wealthy passenger was Benjamin Guggenheim. His fortune had been made in the mining and smelting industry, and he was travelling with his valet, and with his mistress, the French singer Ninette Aubart, while his chauffeur travelled in Second Class. Isador Straus was a partner in the hugely successful Macy's department store in New York; he and his wife Ida were returning from a European holiday. Many of the men of First Class were successful businessmen, but a wide variety of other professions were also represented, including those of artist, jeweller and engineer. Others had made their careers in the military. A significant number of men in First Class were of independent means.[52]

Perhaps even more than for women of the time, the wardrobes of these men were governed by strict rules, many of which were inherited from the socially rigid Victorian era. Although some of these conventions were beginning to be broken down (especially in America), men of wealth

44 Bedroom of First Class suite B57 on *Titanic*.

and influence were expected to show a respectable and formal appearance to the world. As such, all but the most bohemian tended to conform to established modes. A subtle, muted and neat appearance was seen as the socially acceptable ideal, and in comparison to female clothing of the period, variation in style, cut and colour was extremely limited. In this climate of uniformity quality was crucial, and the smallest details mattered. The trained eye could pick up subtle differences in cut, fabric and fit, which made all the difference to a man's public image. However, just as with women's fashions, change was in the air, and new and important innovations were emerging, especially amongst the young. These would have lasting influence on male fashions right up to the present day.

The day started with breakfast, either in the magnificent dining saloon, or in private, in one's stateroom or suite. Despite coming from privileged backgrounds and being used to luxury, First Class passengers reported very favourable impressions of their accommodation, which far exceeded expectations. In a letter written at the start of the voyage the American artist Francis Millet wrote:

> The rooms...are larger than the ordinary hotel rooms and much more luxurious with wooden bedsteads, dressing tables, hot and cold water, etc., etc., electric fans, electric heater and all. The suites with their damask hangings and mahogany oak furniture are really very sumptuous and tasteful. I have the best room I have ever had on a ship and it isn't one of the best either, a great long corridor in which to hang my clothes and a square window as big as the one in the Studio alongside the large light. No end of furniture, cupboards, wardrobe, dressing table, couch etc., etc., not a bit like going to sea.[53]

Upon waking, the gentleman travelling First Class put on a dressing gown over his nightwear. Such gowns were usually made from plain silk for summer, but for the cooler climate expected on board, the alternatives of wool or quilted silk were more appropriate. Braid around collars and pockets was acceptable, as well as some frogging elsewhere. Slippers of matching material were worn, and, for the showier individual, both slippers and dressing gown were monogrammed.

Since all First Class cabins included washbasins, male passengers were able to shave themselves, or have their valet perform this service, if travelling with one. Alternatively, once dressed, a gentleman could visit the on-board barber's shop. Moustaches were fashionable for young men, and older men might sport neatly trimmed beards.

It was now necessary to dress in an appropriate manner for the day ahead, with the help of a valet or male room steward. Since the *Titanic* was heading into a cooler climate, and many First Class passengers would have anticipated enjoying bracing deck-based pursuits, warm underwear was essential. The most popular choice for this was a pair of combinations (also called a union suit). This garment had been part of male clothing since the late nineteenth century, and its purpose was to provide warmth and comfort with the minimum of bulk, since men's clothing, in line with that worn by women, had become more streamlined by this date. Very plain in appearance, and white or cream in colour, combinations were normally made from knitted wool, or a mixture of silk and wool, and clung to the body quite snugly. An opening at the centre front extended from the neck right down the body and was closed with buttons. The sleeves were long, and the legs reached to the ankles. An alternative was to wear separates consisting of a vest and long drawers (later called long johns). Those not requiring a high level of warmth might choose the new short-sleeved vests, available in wool, cotton or spun silk, as well as shorter drawers. T-shirts, which started out as underwear in America during the early twentieth century, were another good alternative to the traditional long-sleeved vest.

Formal Morning Wear

For male clothing during this period, there was a clear distinction between men of different ages and backgrounds, even within First Class. This was something that contemporaries were very conscious of, and in an article in the November 1912 issue of *The Sartorial Art Journal*, an American trade magazine for tailors, the point is made that male fashions 'are sharply divided into two classes, those worn by the conservative man...and those which naturally

45 (opposite) Morning Dress, from T.H. Holding, *Coats*, 1902.

Morning Coats.

are suited to the younger generation who go in for more striking and original novelties'.[54] For smart city dress, formal morning wear, which consisted of a morning suit with a top hat, was still worn, and a few members of the older generation might have taken this option aboard *Titanic*. The morning coat was single breasted, with fronts curving away below the waist and long tails. An even more traditional option was a double-breasted frock coat, which was worn instead of the morning coat, often over a double-breasted waistcoat. Narrow pinstriped trousers were the accepted choice for leg wear, and a white cotton or linen shirt, with detachable stiff linen collar and cuffs, was worn under the coat. In addition to a top hat, cravat and gloves, a cane, and half boots with fabric uppers were the standard accessories. White spats were worn with the smartest outfits.

Informal Day Wear: the Lounge Suit

Although the morning suit was still a part of the male wardrobe of the period, most gentlemen on board wore less formal attire. Surviving photographs of passengers aboard *Titanic* show men in First Class wearing lounge suits. These first emerged as informal wear during the 1870s, but had become increasingly widespread as the standard choice for general day wear and travel during the Edwardian period. King Edward VII himself had been a strong influence on the popularity of this trend. The late king had been an accepted arbiter of style, and was particularly known for his adoption of the single-breasted lounge suit, cut to fasten high on the chest. America, too, was emerging as an important source of new trends. Although English tailors were still acknowledged as the best in the world, America was beginning to take a much greater role in the dissemination of male fashions, leading the way in devising new innovations, and spearheading the march towards greater informality.

Traditional British reserve, however, ensured that American trends were taken up only slowly in the U.K.

Before discussing the lounge suit in more detail, we should explore the other articles of clothing that formed part of this outfit. After putting on his vest and drawers, or combinations, the male passenger of First Class slipped a carefully laundered cotton or linen shirt over his head. Flannel shirts were also an acceptable alternative during cold weather. Shirts were not buttoned all the way down the front during this period; instead the opening reached only to mid chest level. For day wear, the shirt was soft-fronted (as opposed to the stiff-fronted dress shirts which were worn for evening), and fastened with buttons. The usual colour was white, but striped shirts were making an appearance at this time, especially in American wardrobes. As with formal morning dress, men wore detachable stiff linen collars and cuffs with their shirts, a style which was almost universal at the time, but which must have been extremely uncomfortable. Vita Sackville-West, in her novel *The Edwardians,* describes what it might have felt like to wear such a collar. Her character George, whose 'collars were always too high for him and his bowler hat too small...fixed Sylvia very hard with his gaze, and kept swallowing, so that the Adam's apple in his throat bulged uncomfortably against his collar and made him cough two or three times in a way which appeared to annoy him.'[55]

Collars and cuffs were attached with studs, often of bone or ivory, but also made in other materials such as gold, silver or mother-of pearl, with brass or gold fittings. Collar studs, which came in pairs, consisted of a shank, with a large disc at one end to sit next to the skin, and a smaller disc at the other end to slip although the shirt and collar. One was positioned at the back of the neck, and had a shorter shank (since it only had to go through one layer each of shirt and collar), while the other was longer, and designed

46 Men's lounge suits, *Sartorial Art Journal*, June 1904.

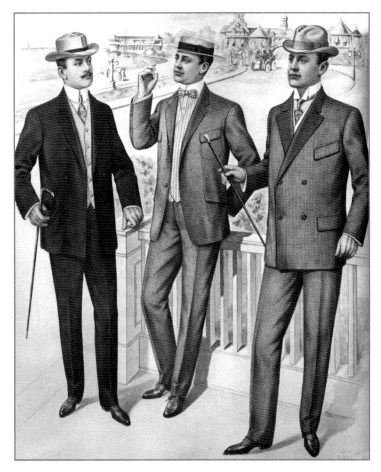

to push through the two holes either side of the neck opening of the shirt, as well as both those on the front of the collar. This closed the shirt at the neck and secured the slightly overlapping collar at the front. Collars themselves varied in style according to personal preference and the types of clothes they accompanied. The unfolded variety, which extended right up to the chin during the Edwardian period, might still be worn by the older generation during the day, but was more likely to be seen with evening wear. The double collar, which folded down with a sharp crease at the top and featured angled or curved fronts to reveal the neckwear beneath, was commonly worn with lounge suits, as was the wing collar, a high single collar on which the curved or pointed corners were folded back under the chin. When the cuffs had been fixed into position, they were joined together with silver or gold cuff links, which for day wear were usually quite plain.

A necktie was secured around the collar, and although black was common, colour was creeping in, either for the whole tie or in the form of diagonal stripes. Narrow ties, which produced a very small knot, were particularly fashionable with lounge suits during this period. However, the less fashionable still adhered to thicker neckties, sometimes embellished with a stud, jewelled or otherwise, at the centre of the knot or just beneath it. The late King Edward VII, who preferred a larger knot, had favoured this thicker style of tie. Some, especially on festive, light-hearted occasions such as informal parties or day trips, also wore patterned or plain bow ties.

Wool socks were worn for day, black, brown or another muted tone, according to the colour of the suit. However, once again, members of the younger or faster set were branching out into brighter colours and patterns. The 1913 catalogue for the Army and Navy stores contains a variety of options for men's socks, including hand-knitted ones made from cashmere or merino wool.[56] In order to present a neat appearance, the majority of wealthier men wore their socks with sock suspenders: adjustable, elasticated straps that were buckled around the calf. A leather section at the front supported a clip, similar to that found on women's suspenders, which attached to the sock, ensuring that the latter would stay wrinkle-free for the entire day. Sock suspenders were to remain in general use right up until the Second World War, and are still worn by some carefully dressed men today.

Having donned his underwear and shirt, our male First Class passenger was now ready to get into his suit. Although the ready-to-wear industry was starting to flourish during this period, the wealthy man scorned such an economy, and instead purchased bespoke suits. His attitude towards the ready-to-wear industry probably matched those expressed in several advertisements from American tailors' establishments reprinted in *The Sartorial Art Journal.* One such advert reads:

> Don't think you are economizing by denying yourself a nice tailored suit and wearing a ready-made suit. It doesn't pay. One of my suits, while it costs a little more at first than the ready-made, is so substantially tailored of the best materials that it will wear, hold its shape and look well after the ready-made is discarded. It more than makes up in style, wear and comfort for the small increase in cost over the ready-made.[57]

London's Savile Row experienced a golden age in the years leading up to the First World War, and was acknowledged as the home of the best makers and suppliers of men's wear in the world. Establishments such as Henry Poole produced the ultimate in men's tailoring, with every suit made to the customer's exact specifications, using only the best materials and long-trusted cutting, stitching and pressing techniques. After the sinking, the inconvenience of the loss of clothing was felt by several of *Titanic*'s male First Class survivors, some of whom were forced to rely on ready-made suits in the days immediately following the disaster—a compromise they were totally unaccustomed to making. Judith Geller, in her book *Titanic, Women and Children First*, cites an article from the *Sturgis Times Democrat* about *Titanic* survivors and First Class passengers Helen Walton Bishop and her husband. It states: 'They expect to remain in New York a week, replenishing their wardrobes. Mrs Bishop playfully referred to her husband's ready-made suit, which had been purchased as an emergency outfit.'[58]

47 (opposite) Man's three-piece lounge suit of dark grey wool with herringbone pattern, c.1891–1901.

In Britain suit trousers were worn fairly fitted and narrow in the leg at this date, although once again American taste differed, with looser, more comfortable styles favoured. Since the 1890s they had been ironed with a crease down the centre, and might either have turn-ups or not, depending on personal taste. Turn-ups were a relatively new fashion and met with disapproval in some quarters. King George V was notoriously conservative in matters of dress, and in her book *The Perfect Summer*, Juliet Nicolson writes 'George loathed turn-ups, thinking that they looked as if a man had rolled up his trousers to keep the hems out of a puddle. If his son appeared wearing them he would ask, with raised eyebrow, "Is it raining in here?"'[59] Trousers extended slightly higher than the natural waistline, often with an adjustable strap at the back for accuracy of fit. They had a button fly, and most featured buttons on the front and back waistband for braces. Belts were beginning to appear at this date, but were not part of general wear for many years to come. Men's braces were one of the few articles for which a certain amount of colour was widely acceptable. They might be of bright colours such as reds or greens, and striped braces were particularly popular. Made either elasticated or from webbing, they had leather sections at the ends with button-holes. At the front, braces were attached to the trouser waistband on either side of the body, but at the back the two straps converged diagonally across the shoulder blades to meet in the middle of the back, whence a single strap passed down to the waistband, and ended in a two-pronged leather attachment with button-holes, that fastened on to two buttons set close together at the back of the trousers.

The waistcoat was the next item to be added to the ensemble. Many of these were made in the same fabric as the jacket and trousers: three-piece suits had first emerged during the 1860s, and remained the prevailing and accepted mode. However, this later period did see the adoption of subtly different types of waistcoat under the jacket, usually of a colour or pattern that toned with the suit. The waistcoat worn with a lounge suit tended to be single-breasted and cut high to the chest, so that it was visible when the jacket was buttoned. Some had narrow revers, but many did not. The waistcoat extended down to waist level, completely obscuring the braces, but rather than being cut straight across the bottom, it was generally angled very gently down towards the centre front. The back of the waistcoat was usually finished with silk satin, and featured an adjustable strap for fit. Linings were of cotton or silk.

Shoes, rather than boots, were normally worn with lounge suits. These were usually quite narrow, with oval-shaped toes, laces, and heels of approximately one inch in height. The best were hand made by firms such as Lobb, which kept wooden lasts for regular clients. Most of the men of First Class would have paid particular attention to the smartness of their appearance, and the cleanliness of shoes was crucial to this. They had to be immaculately clean and shiny, an effect achieved through the services of one's valet or one of the ship's stewards.

Unlike the Norfolk jacket, which was worn for sport and outdoor pursuits, the lounge suit jacket was not belted at the waist. Although double-breasted jackets were also worn at this time, 1912 ushered in a fashion for fairly long, single-breasted versions, which reached well below hip level. Relatively wide lapels, a deep 'V' at the chest, and three buttons to fasten, were common features, but these and other details, such as the number of pockets, could change according to the preferences of the wearer. This was especially true of suits worn by men from the upper levels of society, since individual tailoring catered to the needs of the client in a way that mass-production could not. Suit fabrics were usually made in muted shades of wool, which could feature subtle stripes. Once again, bolder colours were seen in America, and in its November 1912 issue, *The Sartorial Art Journal* states that 'for sack suits [known as lounge suits in Britain] mixture patterns in which green effects predominate are also very considerably in demand, with grey and blue combinations in almost equal favour'.[60] Tweed was also a popular choice, especially that with the traditional herringbone pattern, although some felt the patterns to be too bold. Harris tweed was famous for its durability and was popular with the older generation. In *Clothes and the Man,* the Major explains that Harris tweed is:

> made in the Island of Harris and in the part of Scotland near it...The genuine Harris tweed...is almost waterproof. If you are wearing a suit and it comes on to rain, you will find when you get home that you can shake nearly all the water off the coat. I know that Harris tweeds have been objected to because of their patterns and colourings, which are rather loud...[but] there is a kind of rough-and-ready-look about the patterns which you cannot help liking when you get used to it.[61]

Jacket linings were selected according to the preference of the wearer; flannel was used, as well as striped cotton, and silk might feature in the best suits.

Hats

A man would never have left his sleeping quarters without a hat of some description. It was an absolutely essential accessory, and gentlemen had several styles to choose from. Although top hats were still worn with the formal morning dress suit or frock coat, the common choice of hat to wear with a lounge suit was a bowler. Bowler hats first appeared during the 1840s, worn as protective head wear by gamekeepers. Their popularity as an everyday hat steadily increased during the nineteenth century, and by the pre-

48 Man's bowler hat c.1900–20, made from black wool felt by Lincoln, Bennett & Co.

First World War period they were ubiquitous. With their rounded crown and snug fit they were an excellent choice for travel, since they were comfortable, and rarely blew off, even when the wearer was out promenading on deck in stiff sea breezes.

Another option for informal wear was the cap. These were available in a variety of different styles and sizes, and were initially worn only for sporting activities such as shooting or golfing. However, by the time *Titanic* sailed they were becoming part of everyday wear. One reason for this was the advent of the motorcar. This new and exciting mode of transport had precipitated the development of a whole new range of clothing to protect the wearer from the weather, dust and mud. Included in this was the motoring cap, more generous in cut than an ordinary cap, and worn by both men and women. Although becoming more and more visible on the streets, cars were still the preserve of the very wealthy. Wearing an item of clothing associated with such a prestigious possession, even if one did not actually own one, carried connotations of wealth and privilege, and motoring caps soon found their way into general fashion, particularly in America.

49 Men's overcoats, *Sartorial Art Journal*, December 1909.

Felt hats with turned up brims, and a silk grosgrain ribbon around the crown, were also frequently worn at this time. Types that are still familiar to us today are the Homburg and the Trilby. Edward VII had popularized the Homburg hat during his reign. This was made from stiffened felt, with a fixed dent running down the centre of the crown. The brim was also fixed into position. The Trilby was a soft felt hat, the brim and crown of which could be shaped to some extent by the wearer. The Army and Navy Stores catalogues of the time show that there were many other subtly different versions of these two hat types with names such as The Rutland, The Scarboro', and The Austrian. Colour and fabric finish were sometimes all that distinguished one style from another, but most came in colours such as black, dark brown, olive green and grey.[62] Straw boaters were also popular, but these were more suitable for warmer weather.

Outdoor Wear

If he intended to enjoy a bracing walk along the ship's promenade decks, the First Class gentleman needed further protection. The most popular type of overcoat during this period was the Chesterfield. This was a plain, single-breasted coat that extended to below the knees. The lapels were of medium width (and could incorporate a velvet collar), the buttons were concealed beneath a flap, and the main body was fairly roomy to allow for comfort when walking. Other types of coat with minor variations on the style of the Chesterfield were also available, such as the Ulster or the Victor, and the Inverness incorporated a cape over the shoulders. Double-breasted coats were also worn, and, for a more luxurious touch, wide astrakhan fur collars. Raincoats, cut along the same lines as overcoats in tightly woven textiles such as Gabardine, were worn for wet weather. Leather gloves in a muted colour completed the gentleman's outdoor outfit.

Dressing for Sport

Titanic boasted a variety of sports facilities for use by the men of First Class. These included the gymnasium, squash racquet court, swimming bath and Turkish baths, all of which were novelties on ocean liners.[63] The gymnasium catered for a burgeoning interest in personal fitness and a newly recognized need to cut down on obesity. It contained traditional exercise equipment such as a punch bag, as well as rowing machines, and cycling and riding machines.[64] There were no garments made specifically for wearing in a gym at this time: instead, for aerobic exercise, men wore clothing similar to lighter types of underwear, that is, round-necked vests of cotton jersey or flannel, and cotton trunks or shorts, cut fairly loosely and extending to just above the knee. Occasionally longer trousers were worn.

Swimwear for men was slightly more fitted to the body than that of women, since modesty was not such a great concern for them. It usually consisted of two pieces: a tunic or vest, and trunks. The tunic had short sleeves, and the trunks were cut just above the knee. Decoration, in the form of colourful striped tape at the sleeves, trunk hems and waist, was often seen, and this broke up the otherwise plain, dark fabric, normally wool serge or jersey, that was used for the main parts of the garment.

DRESSING FOR DINNER AND THE EVENING

Allowing a reasonable time before the bugle call for dinner, the men of First Class retired to their rooms to change. Whether taken in the First Class dining saloon or the à la carte restaurant, dinner was an extremely formal affair, requiring full evening dress for both sexes. Those who lived in large houses with numerous domestic staff were used to dressing for dinner as a nightly routine, and it was an expected part of the theatre of an evening meal in *Titanic*'s First Class. Perhaps even more than day wear, the style of men's evening dress was narrowly prescribed. Most men adhered to long-standing sartorial rules and did not deviate from tradition. Only a few of the more daring were beginning to embrace change.

The typical ensemble included a dress shirt, with a cotton, linen or silk body. This was slipped on over the

50 Man in a racing punt, 1913, wearing standard clothing for sport at this time. A tattoo can be seen on his upper arm.

head. It had a stiffened bib front of cotton piqué, which might incorporate fine cords, or feature a diamond pattern weave. This was the prevailing style, but the most modern young men might opt for a soft pleated or tucked shirt, (incorporating an un-stiffened bib front), of the kind just beginning to be worn with evening clothes in fashionable quarters. The *Sartorial Art Journal* stated that the 'plaited or ruffled shirt [was] naturally associated with youth, with daring and the gay *insouciance* of the roistering blade'.[65] Shirts were closed with three studs, rather than buttons. These could be of ivory, in order to tone with the body of the shirt, but might otherwise be of

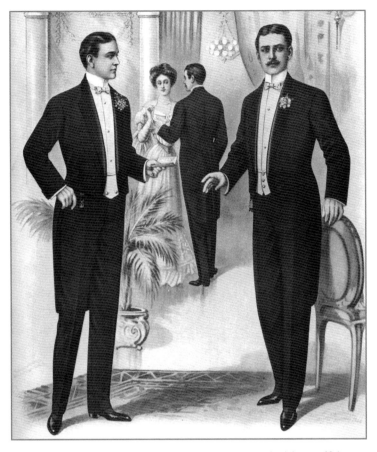

gold or silver, or even be jewelled. Detachable stiff linen cuffs were also fixed in place with studs, and worn with cuff links of a more elaborate style than those worn for day. A narrow white bow tie was tied around a stiff linen collar, and always tied by hand rather than bought ready-made. Ready-made ties were strongly disapproved of: in the 1900 etiquette book *Clothes and the Man*, men were advised to prevent their tie from having 'a stiff sort of appearance' as it would 'look very like a made-up tie. Of course no gentleman ever does wear a made-up tie, and doesn't want the credit of wearing one'.[66]

The trousers for evening dress were quite generously cut, to allow for comfort when sitting at table. They had

52 Men's evening dress including overcoats, canes and top hats. The dinner jacket is shown in the centre. *Sartorial Art Journal*, December 1905.

a buckle at the back of the waist for adjustment of fit, and some had a band of velvet ribbon running down the side. They were always black, and made of fine woven wool. Just as with day wear trousers, they were worn with braces. Socks for evening wear were usually of silk, and clipped into sock suspenders. Black was the accepted norm, but decorated socks were available too, and these had embroidered fronts with simple spotted or striped designs. Footwear was always black, and patent leather shoes with buttoned cloth tops were recommended. Patent leather dance pumps were reserved for wear at balls.

After the trousers were fastened in place, the waistcoat was added. White cotton piqué was standard, but black was

53 Smoking jacket, from T. H. Holding, *Coats*, 1902.

also acceptable. The waistcoat might be single or double breasted according to taste. It was cut with a wide neck to show off the bib-front of the shirt, with the revers narrow, or even completely absent. It fastened with two or three buttons, and was adjustable at the back.

For formal dress, the tailcoat was worn. This was made in the same fabric as the trousers, and the tails reached to just above the backs of the knees. The lapels were wide, and often embellished with black silk. The front of the coat sat open to reveal the waistcoat beneath. It finished at the waistline, with the hem cut to the same level as the bottom of the waistcoat. The coat would be carefully brushed to ensure that it was free of lint and dust. Although the tailcoat was still the usual wear for evening dress, the slightly less formal dinner jacket was beginning to make its mark in fashionable male wardrobes. Called the tuxedo in America, it was increasingly worn on less important occasions, and might well have made an appearance at *Titanic* dinner tables. However, it was still frowned upon by traditionalists, and the official advice was to avoid this garment at evening events whenever women were to be present. It was felt to be more suitable for gentlemen's clubs, men's dinners, or dining at home.

To complete the evening outfit, a few more accessories were needed. These included white kid leather gloves, a muffler or scarf of knitted silk (especially on chilly evenings aboard *Titanic*), and a black silk top hat. An overcoat was worn over the top, a popular choice being a smart, black, streamlined version of the Chesterfield, embellished with silk or velvet lapels.

After dinner, some repaired to the ship's reception rooms or to the First Class lounge. Many played bridge, a common pastime of the upper classes at this period, to the strains of the ship's orchestra. The smoking room was another popular place for male passengers to retire to after

54 Artist's impression (1911) of the First Class smoking room on board *Olympic*.

dinner. In his letter written aboard *Titanic*, Francis Millet specifically mentions this room, which was for men only. He states that there was also one for ladies (probably the reading and writing room), 'I fancy to keep the women out of the men's smoking room which they infest in the German and French steamers'.[67] In order to keep his tailcoat from taking on the smell of tobacco, a gentleman might first have retired to his quarters in order to change into his smoking jacket, also sometimes worn in the afternoon at the same time as a woman might put on her tea gown. The smoking jacket was designed for relaxation, and was frequently made in black velvet, generally with a silk shawl collar, and often decorated with frogging or braid around the collar, cuffs and pockets. Dark wood panelling, leather chairs, and a working fireplace were features of the First Class smoking room aboard *Titanic*. They helped to create the rarified atmosphere of this exclusively male space.

Eventually the men of First Class retired to their cabins, and, their many layers of clothing at last removed, slipped into their pyjamas and their comfortable beds. Pyjamas had first begun to rival the nightshirt or long chemise as bed wear from the late nineteenth century, and had now become ubiquitous. They were made of either silk, cotton or flannel according to the weather, and the pocket and tastes of the wearer, and came in a variety of colours and patterns.

Approximately 173 men were travelling First Class aboard *Titanic;* only 54 of them survived the disaster. Col. Astor was refused a place in a lifeboat alongside Madeleine, but was commended for his bravery in helping many others to safety. Benjamin Guggenheim was helped into his life-belt by a steward, who also made him put on a thick sweater to go on deck. However, according to the steward, who survived, Guggenheim returned to his cabin, and changed into his evening dress, along with his valet, saying 'We've dressed up in our best and are prepared to go down like gentlemen.'[68] When Isador Straus was refused permission to board a lifeboat with his wife Ida, she chose to remain with him, and both lost their lives in the sinking. Francis Millet, the letter writer, also drowned. As his body was recovered, we know that he was wearing evening dress of black trousers and a grey jacket, a light overcoat, a gold watch and chain, and two gold studs.

5. Followers of Fashion: Second and Third Class Passengers

As WE MARVEL AT the opulent surroundings, lifestyles and clothing of *Titanic's* First Class passengers, it is easy to forget that these privileged individuals were considerably outnumbered by passengers with cheaper tickets, who did not travel in such comfort. Two hundred and eighty-five people travelled Second Class, whilst no less than 710 embarked as Third Class passengers. While the shipping companies offered great luxury on the upper decks, and charged accordingly, they actually profited most from the sheer numbers of people who travelled in Third Class. Without their custom, the magnificent liners built during the early years of the twentieth century would not have been economically viable. Competition to win this lucrative market meant that Third Class accommodation had improved beyond measure since the 'coffin ships' of the 1840s, and the designers of the *Titanic* had taken particular care to ensure that the needs and expectations of Third Class passengers were met and often exceeded. Second Class accommodation was also comparatively luxurious, and was said to rival that of First Class in many existing ships.

Second Class passengers were crossing the Atlantic for a variety of reasons. Some, such as Mr Reginald Charles Coleridge, were travelling as part of their work. As a British

advertising consultant, he was making his way to Detroit, Michigan on business, but never got there.[69] Some were on holidays or trips to see friends and family. This group included survivors 8-year-old Marshall Drew and his aunt and uncle, James and Lulu Drew, who were returning to New York after a trip to visit family in Cornwall.[70] Many were emigrating to America from Britain in order to start a new life, often planning to meet up with family or friends who had already established themselves successfully. Harvey Collyer, with his wife Charlotte and daughter Marjorie, was travelling to Payette, Idaho in order to become a fruit farmer. Charlotte and Marjorie escaped with their lives but nothing else, as when Harvey drowned he was carrying all their money in cash, including the proceeds of the sale of their business.[71] Thomas Brown, whose Cape Town hotel business had declined, with his wife and their daughter Edith, was moving to a new continent in order to start afresh in the favourable American economic climate. He put them into a lifeboat with the words 'I'll see you in New York.' Alas, he never did, and they returned to South Africa without him. Edith lived to be 100 years old, and, in 1993, to be presented with her father's gold watch, recovered from the wreck. She died in 1997, in Southampton, the city from which she had embarked on *Titanic* as a 15-year-old.[72]

Second Class tickets cost abound £12 per person, and the accommodation and facilities, although not as lavish as those of First Class, were still excellent. Particular features were the oak-panelled vestibule that greeted passengers as they boarded through doors embellished with stained glass, and the grand staircase that served all of the Second Class accommodation. Cabins were plainer in style and less spacious than their First Class equivalents, but still provided comforts such as electric lights, wash stands (with manually filled water tanks rather than hot and cold running water), wardrobes and wooden bedsteads. Passengers were

55 (opposite, top) Artist's impression (1912) of the Second Class promenade on the Boat Deck (B Deck) of *Titanic*.

56 (opposite, bottom) Artist's impression (1912) of a Second Class cabin on board *Titanic*.

57 Artist's impression (1911) of the Second Class library on *Olympic*.

impressed with their surroundings and with the sheer size of the ship. Harvey Collyer wrote to his parents while on the first leg of the journey from Southampton to Queenstown: 'Well dears so far we are having a delightful trip the weather is beautiful and the ship magnificent. We can't describe the tables it's like a floating town. I can tell you we do swank we shall miss it on the trains as we go third on them'[73] Facilities included a library, smoking room, barber's shop and attractively decorated dining room where passengers were provided with four meals a day. A five-course Second Class dinner menu for 14 April survives in the collections of the National Maritime Museum: alongside the other rich and generous courses it includes curried chicken, spring lamb and roast turkey.[74]

Those travelling Third Class were most likely to be crossing the Atlantic to start a new life in North America. During the four years before the First World War, the number of people who emigrated to the United States is said to have averaged one million per year. Ellis Island, the New York gateway for all immigrants to America, saw 637,003 people pass through its doors in 1911 alone.[75] Some were travelling on to Canada, which, between 1906 and 1915, welcomed a total of 2,278,396 immigrants, the largest proportion (926,003) of which were from Britain, Ireland and British colonies.[76] Many emigrants, including most of the British, were seeking to escape poverty, unemployment and the limitations of a rigid class system. They wished to improve their prospects in a strengthening economy that was said to offer opportunity for all. Although the greatest number of people travelling Third Class aboard *Titanic* were from Britain and Ireland, other nationalities were also represented. The next largest group had travelled to Cherbourg or Southampton from Scandinavia, and countries such as Austro-Hungary, Syria, Bulgaria and Russia were also represented.[77] Many of those travelling from Syria and from Russian-occupied states such as Finland were fleeing religious and political persecution. Sadly, only 174 out of the 710 people travelling Third Class would survive the disaster.

Members of Third Class included Emily and Frank Goldsmith, and their son Frank, who was nine years old. They planned to travel to Detroit, Michigan, where members of Emily's family had already settled. Frank senior was a toolmaker, and Emily a seamstress. Their skills should have helped to secure them work when they reached their destination. Entire families were making their way across the Atlantic, many with all their worldly goods stowed in the hold of the ship. The Andersson family from Sweden consisted of Alfrida and Anders and their five children, Sigrid, Ingeborg, Ebba, Sigvard and Ellis. They were bound for Winnipeg, Canada, where they hoped to establish themselves as farmers, but the whole family was lost in the sinking. Many of those travelling were young women who had secured positions as servants in American households.

Amongst these was Amy Stanley, from Oxfordshire, who was due to work for the Dann family in New Haven, Connecticut, and was among those fortunate enough to reach their destination safely.[78] Others were travelling to meet their intended husbands.

The ship's Third Class accommodation was basic, but fairly comfortable in comparison to provision aboard earlier ships. It may also have been an improvement on the conditions that many passengers were used to at home. Cabins and public areas were on the lower decks of the ship, and unlike the sleeping quarters in many other vessels during this period, all Third Class accommodation consisted of cabins rather than larger dormitories. The number of berths varied from two to ten. The cheapest cabins were designated for men only, and tended to have the largest number of berths. There were other areas allocated to single women and families. Tickets cost between £3 and £8 per person, and the men only cabins were basic and very sparse. They had metal bunks, fixed to the walls, and, unlike other Third Class cabins, they had no washbasins. The mattresses were filled with straw and the only bed covering provided was a White Star Line blanket. The better Third Class cabins included washbasins and proper bed linen. There were no wardrobes: only hooks on the wall for clothing. In the Third Class dining saloon passengers ate at long wooden tables with white tablecloths, served by uniformed stewards. They did not have to bring their own food, a common requirement in earlier ships, but were served a generous and varied menu. Dishes included steak-and-kidney pie, ragout of beef, fish, rabbit, fresh vegetables and puddings. Fresh fruit, freshly baked bread and butter were also provided. For some, these may have been the most plentiful and nutritious meals they had ever eaten. There was a Third Class men's smoking room, and a general room for socializing and relaxation. Passengers also had access to open deck areas for fresh air and exercise.

The clothing of Second and Third Class passengers varied greatly according to sex, age, financial circumstances and cultural background. Dress was much more costly than it is today, but, at almost every level of society, certain basic conventions and rules of etiquette were adhered to. Strongly held concepts of decency meant that women wore long skirts (ankle length or below), despite their cumbersome nature and their tendency to become dirty at the hem. Men always wore caps or hats out of doors, etiquette dictating that these should be removed when indoors and, especially in the case of boys, doffed in the presence of social superiors. Many of those who travelled Second Class had a certain amount of disposable income, and although they may not have been at the cutting edge of style, they were able to afford relatively fashionable clothes of good quality. Made-to-measure, home-made, as well as limited ready-to-wear, were all options, and retailers were increasingly aiming their products at those whom today we would describe as middle class. It

58 Artist's impression (1912) of the Third Class smoking room on board *Titanic*.

59 A Sunday School outing, c.1909–12. Everyone is wearing their Sunday best.

made good business sense, since in Britain, and most other western countries, this group made up a large proportion of the population. Even in Third Class, the majority of people would have been dressed in decent clothing. The White Star Line claimed to be targeting a 'better class of immigrant', and the cost of a Third Class ticket excluded the very poor. Many of those on their way to America were skilled workers, with trades that provided them with enough money to meet basic clothing requirements.

The clothing of poorer members of society is generally more difficult to document, since very little of it survives in museums. What ordinary people were wearing on *Titanic*, especially as outerwear, is directly attested from photographs taken on the voyage, and we can extrapolate further details from general photographs of the period, and from oral history accounts that mention the ways dress was acquired and worn in Britain and neighbouring countries. While we cannot be certain what travellers from countries further away wore, elements of traditional costume from Scandinavian and Southern Mediterranean cultures would certainly have been seen on board. Exact if somewhat macabre evidence for what people were wearing on the night of the sinking is to be had from the descriptions of bodies retrieved for burial by the ship *Mackay Bennett*. These include detailed records of clothing, made to aid identification.[79]

Following Fashion

Contemporary photographs of ordinary people show women wearing smart, fitted clothing and accessories along the lines of the general fashionable look of the high Edwardian period, whilst men's clothes also have elements that resemble those of their wealthier counterparts. The historian must, however, be slightly wary, since these images were almost always taken on special occasions when people would have been dressed in their Sunday best rather than their everyday working clothing. Nevertheless, they are a true record, and make a very good starting point for analysing the types of clothing that the passengers of Second and Third Class wore aboard *Titanic*.

Up until this period, the concept of fashion, as opposed to simple, functional clothing, had generally been the preserve of the upper classes. The latest styles were dictated by the aristocracy and limited to those who had the time and money for costly purchases and multiple fittings. During the Edwardian period this had begun to change, and new developments in popular culture, and the greater affordability of dress, meant that a growing proportion of the population

60 Enjoying a day of sport, c.1912–14.

was now able to follow fashion. Although members of the aristocracy and the royal family were still considered leaders in some areas of fashion, a new and much more accessible influence on fashion was gathering momentum: that of popular culture. The cult of celebrity had its roots in the Edwardian period. Fashion trends were now as likely to be set by stage actresses such as Camille Clifford, Eva Moore and Maxine Elliott, who were of course dressed by the leading couturiers of the day. As mentioned in chapter 2, stage beauty Lily Elsie is said to have popularized the wide-brimmed and heavily trimmed Edwardian hat designed by Lady Duff Gordon. Even if women were not able to see these actresses on stage, cheap postcards with photographic portraits of them were widely available. In addition, articles in women's magazines were giving increasing coverage to their style of dress, and, for that matter, to fashion in general. Even daily newspapers were running articles on fashion, reflecting the growing popular interest in the subject. All these things fuelled the fashion aspirations of ordinary people, and the market responded in a variety of ways.

The increasing availability of cheaper yet fashionable clothing meant that it was easier for those on lower incomes to emulate the dress of the better-off, even if only superficially. The extension of access to fashion beyond the world of wealth and privilege, and the consequent potential for social mobility, was not universally welcomed; indeed it was criticized and even mocked. Gertrude Jekyll, in her 1904 commentary on the traditions and clothing of the working people of rural West Surrey, lamented the more general adoption of fashionable dress: 'Now, alas! all workpeople... are clothed in a dead-level of shabbiness. The shops are full of cheap suits with a pretence of fashion'. She also comments scathingly on the dress of a rural wedding party which was attempting to emulate the dress of the wealthy:

> The bride had a veil and orange blossoms, a shower bouquet and *pages!* The bridegroom wore one of the cheap suits aforesaid, and had a billycock hat pushed back from his poor, anxious, excited face that glistened with sweat. In his button-hole was a large bouquet, and on his hands *white cotton gloves!* No more pitiful exhibition could well be imagined. Have these poor people so utterly lost the sense of the dignity of their own position that they can derive gratification from the performance of such an absurd burlesque?[80]

Such disapproval did not prevent poorer people from acquiring fashionable dress, and members of *Titanic*'s Third Class were no exception. Indeed, on the night of the sinking, Third Class passenger Amy Stanley, who had been an apprentice dressmaker and worked for fashionable clothing retailers before going into service, was dressed very like a First Class passenger. When the alarm was raised she changed out of her nightwear into a dress of blue silk and donned a fur coat before making her way to the lifeboats. Once aboard the *Carpathia*, her appearance caused her to be mistaken for a member of First Class, and she was shown to a cabin and given a bunk. When it was discovered she was from steerage, she was banished to sleep rough with the rest of the third class survivors.[81]

Acquiring Clothing

For those with a reasonable amount of disposable income, an important source of new fashionable clothing was the department store. These had made their way into most major cities by this period, and included Kendal Milne & Co. in Manchester, Fenwick in Newcastle, and Lewis's in Liverpool, Manchester and Birmingham. Debenham and Freebody, Whiteleys, Harrods, and Selfridges were just a few of the many stores available to shoppers in London. New York also had a glut of similar outlets including Lord & Taylor and Macy's. Indeed, First Class passenger Isidor Straus was, as mentioned, a partner in Macy's. The complicated nature of women's clothing and the lack of standardization in sizing meant that in department stores most items were still made to measure, but the larger scale of production meant that prices were becoming more competitive, at least in some establishments. Others preferred to keep prices high in order to retain a wealthier clientele. Ready-made pieces were available in lines such as coats, skirts, blouses, mantles and underwear, all of which were less fitted, and could more easily accommodate a broad range of figures. The ready-to-wear clothing industry was more advanced in America, which would soon lead the

61 Cover of French fashion magazine *La Nouvelle Mode* showing a fashionable style which could easily be reproduced by a competent dressmaker. March 1912 issue.

world in this field. In addition to made-to-order and ready-made articles, stores experimented with semi-made-up items, which could be finished to the correct size at home. Skirts might be sold ready-made, or with an unmade seam at the back, alongside material for making up the bodice. Peter Robinson offered dresses that could be finished off by stitching up the seam at the back.

Some department stores such as Lewis's targeted people on more moderate incomes. Selfridges, on London's Oxford Street, had a bargain basement and, while cultivating an air of luxury, aimed to provide a non-intimidating atmosphere for those who wished to browse, rendering it a popular tourist destination. Those without access to larger cities were also well catered for. The Army and Navy Stores produced extensive catalogues, which contained every conceivable household item as well as clothing, and offered mail-order services throughout Britain and the world. Army and Navy was at this time a form of co-operative society, which encouraged loyalty and kept prices lower. The Co-op itself had an important impact on the provision of new clothing for the less well off: the cost of becoming a member, although out of reach of the very poorest, was still modest, and at the store ordinary people could buy reasonably priced ready-to-wear items, as well as fabrics to make up. Second Class passengers doubtless purchased some of their clothing from department stores, and some of them, as well as many from Third Class, would have been members of the Co-op.

The making of home-sewn garments, a mainstay for ordinary families, was facilitated by the widespread use of sewing machines and the availability of paper patterns for fashionable clothes. Cheap ready-made clothing, particularly men's wear, was generally available to the poorer members of society by this date, but, sometimes referred to as slop, it still had a reputation for being ill-fitting and made from poor quality fabrics. In preference to this, many Third Class passengers would have acquired some of their clothing second-hand, since the quality could be higher. There had long been a lively trade in second-hand clothing, available from a variety of sources, the main ones being markets. Most large towns had markets with second-hand clothing stalls, and cities such as Liverpool and London had markets dedicated specifically to clothing. Liverpool's Paddy's Market was situated between Scotland Road and Livington Hill, and stallholders stocked almost every type of garment, in varying states of newness or decay. An article by Paul Pry in the *Liverpool Review* in 1884 includes a description of the types of clothing sold: 'bodycoats, frock coats, short coats of the most pattern, petticoats of all sizes, shapes and hues, from the "linsey wolsey" of the locality to the cast-off silk of the tradesman's wife...glaringly coloured handkerchiefs, corduroy breeches, moleskin trousers'.[82] In London, the trade centred around Petticoat Lane market in the East End.

Second-hand clothing shops were also common at this time, as were travelling salesmen who sold clothes. Dealers advertised second-hand clothes by mail-order, as an option for those who lived further away from shopping centres, or those who could not afford to buy new, but who wished to avoid the stigma of purchasing in person. Clothing might also be acquired directly from its original wearers. It was common practice for servants to be offered clothing from the family they were working for, and this might be worn (usually altered to remove trimmings), or sold to dealers to provide extra income. Pawnbrokers provided a further outlet. Some customers pawned their clothing on a Monday, and redeemed it again on Friday or Saturday (pay day) in order to wear it on Sunday. This alternative use of clothing as security for loans provided a vital source of income for many families, but inevitably some garments were never redeemed, and large sales took place.

UNDERWEAR

Corsets were worn at virtually every level of society at this period, except for a few young, daring, high-fashion individuals. Ordinary working women had had access to fashionable foundation wear since the late nineteenth century. Firms such as Symington of Market Harborough had been manufacturing corsets on a large scale in their mechanized factories since the 1880s, and sold many of their lines at extremely competitive prices. Symington's Pretty Housemaid corset, available from around 1890, was advertised as 'the strongest and cheapest corset ever made'. The line was aimed directly at female domestic servants, who at that time constituted the largest proportion of the female working population. Rust-proof spiral steels for boning were developed from 1907. Expensive whalebone was no longer necessary for the production of flexible and wash-proof corsets, and this and other developments meant that cheaper foundation wear could be produced to cater for the needs of women further down the income scale, reducing the need to resort to home-made or second-hand versions.

All the other forms of underwear typical of the Edwardian period were worn by the majority of women too. These included combinations to go under the corset, or separate chemises and drawers. Petticoats were worn, partly to achieve the required silhouette under skirts, but also for warmth. As one might expect, the difference between these undergarments and those of wealthier members of society was the quantity, quality and type of fabric used, and the extent to which they were decorated. Ordinary underwear was made of thick white cotton, wool flannel or wool jersey, with decoration limited according to the tastes and pocket of the wearer. It took the form of pin tucks, ribbons or lace, and cheaper machine-made lace was making this type of embellishment far more accessible to those on limited budgets. Although many undergarments, like outerwear, could be purchased ready-made, or made-to-order from the department stores and co-operative societies, a large proportion were still home-made. They were either hand sewn, or produced with the help of a sewing machine, an article now widely available for hire

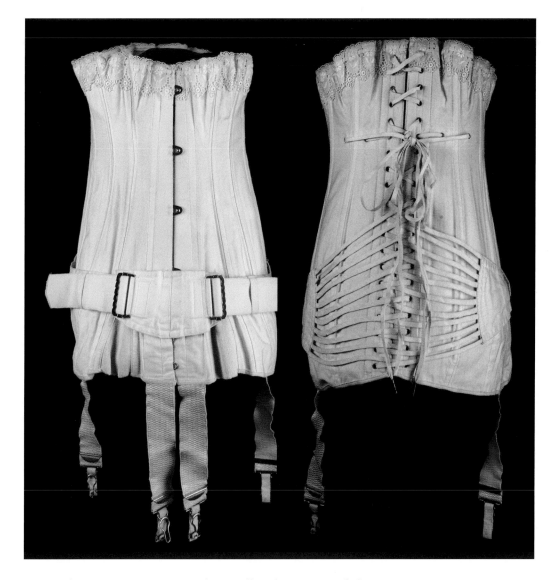

or purchase. Sewing was taught to all girls as part of their education, and was seen as an essential life skill, which women might use to provide clothing for themselves and their families, or, frequently, to earn money. Miss Stella Ann Sage, a 20-year-old travelling in Third Class, was a dressmaker who intended to find work at her destination of Jacksonville, Florida. Emily Goldsmith, also in Third

62 A Jenyns corset from 1911. It has a distinctive belt support designed to give 'increased ease in every position'. During the First World War it was marketed as particularly suitable for for women undertaking war work.

Class, had a prized sewing machine which was packed in the hold and went down with the ship.

For many of those travelling Third Class, underwear was of course worn solely for warmth, and was limited in quantity. There was very little space within cabins to store clothing while on board—just simple clothes hooks—so some passengers might only have had two or three changes of undergarments for the voyage. In the records of the clothing on bodies recovered from the sea by the cable ship *Mackay Bennett*, Third Class female passengers were found wearing woollen underwear such as grey flannel drawers, a flannel vest or chemise and a wool flannel petticoat, plus black or grey wool stockings. Corsets are only occasionally mentioned, but their absence might be explained by the hurry in which many people had to dress as they attempted to escape the sinking ship.

Children in general were well wrapped up. Lena Burton, who came from a working-class family, and went out to work herself from the age of thirteen, mentions the layers of clothes that she wore as a child during the Edwardian period:

> We always wore all sorts of clothes. First a vest, then a chemise over the top, then a liberty bodice, then a flannel petticoat and a cotton petticoat, then your frock, and a pinny over the top. And knickers—and woollen stockings that Mother knitted herself—she used to make all our frocks too. We kids sweltered to death in those days.[83]

Many of the very poorest children at this time had their chests rubbed with fat and were actually sewn into their undergarments for the winter. Others were subjected to even more basic methods to try to keep them warm. Anne Taylor recounts how her Edwardian father would get Russian tallow, 'and he used to rub it on our chests, and since our clothes weren't thick, he'd wrap sheets of brown paper round us.'[84]

Second and Third Class men's underwear is also noted in the *Mackay Bennett* lists, although, as with women's corsets, it is sometimes missing, possibly again because the wearers were forced to dress hurriedly. The items that occur repeatedly are woollen vests (or singlets as they are called in the listings). These are far more numerous than pairs of drawers, but where the latter are mentioned, they tend to be woollen. Wool flannel underwear was also worn, sometimes in the form of men's combinations, the legs for these extending down to mid-calf, as for separate drawers. Socks of grey or black wool are also frequently noted. As with the majority of men's underwear of the period, such items were practical and warm rather than decorative.

OUTERWEAR

Outerwear for Women

Despite recent developments in the lengthening and straightening of the silhouette in high fashion, many ordinary women at this date continued to wear the styles that had dominated fashion since the start of the century, namely long, flaring skirts and tight bodices, fitted to the natural waistline, and requiring solid corsetry. The most common everyday garments for women of the period, especially during the colder months, were generally based on the Tailor-made suit. This neat ensemble of wool skirt and jacket, worn over a blouse, was, as we have noted, extremely popular with women from the upper levels of society, but its practical and hard-wearing nature meant that cheaper versions were also taken up enthusiastically by women from virtually all walks of life. For those who could not afford an entire suit, simple wool skirts with cotton or wool flannel shirts were the most common items worn, with a coat or knitted jacket for warmth. A suit was considered a highly suitable garment for the working woman, whose career and earning opportunities began to broaden at this time. It was

63 Women's fashion magazines of the period often produced paper patterns for readers to order. For most women, home dressmaking was an important and affordable way of keeping fashionably up-to-date. *The Queen, The Lady's Newspaper*, March 1912.

PAPER PATTERN.

A NEW

BLOUSE

Paper pattern of blouse, 1s. 1d., from the *Queen* Office, Bream's Buildings, E.C.

Catalogue will be sent on receipt of 1d. stamp.

also a practical garment for travelling, and examples were undoubtedly seen on the Second and Third Class decks. The differences between the expensive versions of suits (or costumes, as they were often called) and those worn by ordinary women were the cut, style and fabric: wool serge was the most usual material, but other types of woven wool, such as tweed, were also used. Shoddy, a recycled fabric made up from rags, was the most economical textile available, and was widely used in the ready-to-wear industry.

Other garments worn by less wealthy women included simple full-length woollen or cotton dresses, in dark colours during the winter and in lighter shades for warmer weather, with minimal decoration. However, the records of the

Mackay Bennett also indicate that some women, especially those who hailed from mainland Europe and beyond, wore colourful clothes. For example, one unidentified woman stated to be aged about thirty, likely to be from Third Class and of Italian origin, is described as wearing a green cotton blouse, a striped cotton skirt and a blue petticoat.[85] Wendla Maria Heininen, another Third Class passenger, who came from Laitilia, Finland, was wearing a red striped skirt with a green petticoat.[86] While clothing like this was clearly associated with the particular ethnic and cultural backgrounds of the women concerned, they may not have been wearing traditional regional costume as such, but rather clothes with an emphasis on colour, with certain types of decoration that were favoured in their respective cultures.

The women of Second Class, at least those with some money to spend and time to shop, are likely to have followed the latest styles more closely. Eschewing, for the most part, the less practical aspects of extreme trends such as the hobble skirt, they nevertheless opted for garments with fashionable elements. These included high waists, and suits with long, narrow jackets and slender skirts, which incorporated asymmetrical details, tunics or overskirts, and slits and pleats to facilitate walking. These items could be made to order by department stores, or by independent tailors who kept patterns for regular clients. Some passengers might have chosen to save money on less important garments by using local dressmakers, a practice not uncommon even amongst the upper classes. Cynthia Asquith mentions just such a dressmaker in her memoirs:

> Not even my clothes escaped my mother's kindness of heart, for unfortunately for me a charming sometime lady's maid of hers had set up as a dressmaker—the kind of dressmaker whom, whatever her size and bulk, one always calls—in the hope, I suppose, that her *bills* will be little—a 'Little Woman'. Needless to say a large proportion

of my clothes had to be made by this 'Little Woman' who had no models, but only paper patterns. Even my seventeen-year-old unsophisticated eye could see that her clothes were not 'right'.[87]

Warm coats were important for all passengers aboard *Titanic*, and many women wore full-length wool overcoats in loose styles. These were usually of dark colours such as brown, burgundy and black. One such coat, typical of the period in style and construction, was worn by second-class passenger Marion Wright, and survived the disaster along with its owner. It was made from brown wool with a red or purplish tinge, had wide lapels with topstitching, and was double breasted with six brass buttons. The coat reached to the ankles, and extended into an A-line shape to accommodate long skirts beneath. Marion went on to wear it at her marriage to Arthur Woolcott, the man whom she had been travelling to join, on the 20 April 1912.[88] If their budgets did not stretch to a coat, the poorer women of Third Class wore large woollen shawls around their shoulders or over their heads and shoulders. This form of outdoor covering was particularly common amongst working class women from the northern counties of Britain, and also amongst rural communities in Europe. Large shawls, often with brightly coloured designs, had been part of women's wear since the early nineteenth century, and although no longer considered fashionable, were still readily available from various sources and widely worn by less wealthy women.

The addition of fashionable accessories, particularly hats, was an affordable way to update an outfit. Hats were worn outdoors by women of almost every level of society, and contemporary photographs show how flamboyant they could be. The typically wide-brimmed and heavily trimmed hats of the era were enthusiastically adopted by many. For those who could not afford to patronize a milliner, a plain straw or felt hat, made in a fashionably wide style, could be purchased relatively cheaply on the high street. A multitude of different trimmings such as ribbons, artificial flowers, feathers and veiling could be bought from a haberdasher, and the hat trimmed at home. Although high fashion was turning away from the widest hat styles by 1912, they remained very much in evidence in the wardrobes of many women.

Fashionable women's footwear was available off-the-shelf or through mail-order at an affordable cost. An advertisement in the March 1912 issue of *The Queen* magazine offers high-fashion shoe styles for 3s and 9d a pair. Although called the Parisian Shoe Manufacturers, the address given is Loddices Road, Hackney, East London. The advert claims that 'similar quality shoes are being sold in Leading West End Shops at more than double the price we charge'. Traditional cobblers could provide more practical footwear in slightly less up-to-date styles. Leather boots, both fashionable and practical, were worn by many women, and all women's footwear of the period tended to be narrow in the foot. Boots were ankle length, with laces up the front or buttons to the side. For those lower down the income scale, boots were more frequently worn than shoes, as they were warmer, and more suitable for heavy use.

64 Advertisement for 'Parisian shoes', *The Queen, The Lady's Newspaper,* March 1912.

65 Pair of everyday women's lace-up shoes of tan coloured leather with leather soles, c.1900–10.

Pair of women's black glacé leather button boots, with the label 'Bective', c.1900–12.

Outerwear for Children

There were twenty-five children travelling Second Class aboard *Titanic*, considerably more than in First Class, and all of them survived the sinking. Aboard ship these children had to amuse themselves with simple games and toys they had brought themselves, and gathered together to play in the enclosed area of the C-deck promenade, presumably under the supervision of their mothers or older siblings: no nannies are listed as travelling with the Second Class families. The children of Third Class were far more numerous, and most sources agree that there were eighty aboard, only twenty-five of whom survived. Some belonged to large families, and just like the children travelling in First and Second Class, they would have made friends with fellow child passengers as they explored the designated Third Class sections of the ship, no doubt also supervised, when out of sight of their parents, by older siblings, just as they were in the streets back home. The many public areas of the *Titanic* would quickly have become a vast and endlessly fascinating playground.

Second Class children were dressed in smart clothes with outward appearance similar to those worn in First Class. Garments included sailor suits for both boys and girls, simple frocks with below-the-knee length skirts for girls, and suits for boys. However, rather than being made-to-measure by specialist dressmakers or tailors, these would have been sourced ready-made from department stores or smaller retail outlets. Children's wear lent itself more easily to ready-made mass production, since it tended to be less fitted, and although by this period children's clothing followed its own fashion trends, styles changed less quickly than they did for adults. The rapid rate at which children grew out of clothes also meant that for economic reasons, home sewing was common practice even among the middle classes. The dress pattern industry was booming, and dress pattern producers such as Weldon & Co. and Butterick published illustrated catalogues with many designs for children's wear. These simple styles, especially for girl's frocks, meant that mothers or servants with quite limited technical skill could produce garments at home. Much of the clothing worn by the children of Third Class would have been produced in this way, or purchased second-hand.

Frocks were mid-calf or just below the knee in length, the more fashionable featuring a drop-waist, puffed sleeves and a roomy bodice. Wool is likely to have been the most common choice of fabric for young passengers, given the time of year. Pinafores, if worn, were simpler in style than those owned by First Class children, and although decorated with frills and tucks, were less lavishly trimmed with lace and embroidery. For warmth outside, girls in Second Class might be dressed in dark velvet or woollen double breasted coats with wide collars. These were fitted at chest level, falling loosely below, with more fitted styles for older girls. For the better off, fur trimmings were added to collars and cuffs, also small fur muffs, with a

66 An infant school class, c.1910–14.

cord extending around the neck to keep them from getting lost. Matching hats, often tam-o-shanters, were also worn. Alternatives included straw hats with simple trimmings of imitation flowers. Girls wore their hair long, often with a ribbon pulling it back from the face, and curled using rags, or plaited into pigtails. Hair was not worn up until girls were deemed to have reached adulthood in their late teens, at which point they also graduated to longer skirts. Cynthia Asquith recalls her feelings during this transition from girlhood to womanhood:

> The transformation of a child into a young woman was dramatically sudden: yesterday her golden hair was hanging down her back; today it was 'up', coiled into what she called a Grecian knot....Simultaneously the hem of her skirt fell to the ground. I still remember the thrill of hearing the whisper of my first long dress pursuing my heels down the stairs, and the queerness of suddenly no longer being able to see my own feet. I remember too the pang of saying goodbye to that badge of irresponsibility, my pigtail.[89]

Girls travelling in Third Class wore clothing similar to that described above, but of plainer, simpler construction, and made from coarser, cheaper materials with little decoration. They might not have adhered to the latest drop-waist styles, since second-hand or handed-down clothing could be five to ten years old. The clothes of the poorest children were also much mended and patched. However, just as with wealthier members of society, a child's appearance was a source of pride and dignity to parents, and even in the poorer households, much time and effort was devoted to ensuring that children were decently dressed in clean clothes. The prevailing fashion for white clothing for children was widely followed, even by those on meagre incomes, and keeping these items starched and spotless was always a source of much pride and not inconsiderable effort. Washday for working class households with lots of children was a major undertaking, as Annie Swain recalls:

> Everything had to be beautiful with starch. Pillowcases, shirt cuffs, collars, petticoats...Mind, the clothes in those days were white! Sometimes we had to swill six sheets, all the men's shirts, all the chemises with three yards of stuff in every one! Then white knickers, petticoats for the children, which they wore two of every Sunday, and if you had a family of girls you'll understand what it was like, and then the nightdresses all made of calico. We had terrible times in those days, but we were always kept very clean. In those back lanes in those days, it was always to see who had the whitest clothes. It was just like a competition'[90]

Boy's clothing was more uniform than that of girls, and also less varied than that worn by their First Class counterparts. Apart from sailor suits, other forms of boy's suits were of simple, plain styles, in muted grey or dark wool shades or tweeds. Jackets were either of the simple lounge suit variety, echoing that of their fathers, or, very often, in the Norfolk cut with box pleats and a belt. Matching waistcoats

67 Family group c.1910.
The boy on the left wears a
Norfolk suit, a popular choice
for little boys of all classes at
this date.

were frequently worn with lounge-style suits, and beneath these, cotton or flannel shirts. Wealthier boys usually wore detachable, wide, starched white collars, particularly for special occasions. Boys from poorer families are less likely to have worn collars for everyday, although these are often seen in formal photographs, for which of course they were dressed in their best. One oral history account records that collars could be made from paper for the occasion![91] Shorts or knickerbockers were worn by younger boys, who graduated into longer trousers when they reached the age of sixteen. Alfred Rush, a Third Class passenger who was travelling from Southampton to Detroit, Michigan, celebrated his sixteenth birthday on board ship, exchanging his short trousers for long ones. He is said to have relinquished a place in a lifeboat due to his new status as a man.[92] Another form of clothing suitable for cold weather, particularly for boys, was the knitted jersey or Guernsey. Also frequently part of wealthier boys' wardrobes, this was an economical option for the less well off, since it could be knitted at home. Cloth caps were the usual head wear for boys, and these were worn almost universally, even by the poorest children, as they too were expected to adhere to the hat-wearing etiquette of the age.

Shoe styles for girls from Second Class featured a simple bar across the instep, perhaps with a small heel for older girls. However, ankle boots, both buttoned and laced, were also very common for everyday wear, particularly outdoors. Boys and children from less wealthy backgrounds were more likely to wear stout leather boots, in varying states of repair, for the same reasons that their adult counterparts did: they were more hard-wearing. Children's footwear was a particular problem for the very poor, since new pairs were required as the child grew. It was not unknown for some children to go shoeless in the poorest areas, and others had to make do with the wrong sizes or worn out second-hand pairs. Reece Elliott, who grew up in a working class household during the Edwardian period, recalled that:

> In those days we were lucky if we had one pair of boots—no shoes, dear me. Many a time we walked with two odd uns. People who were well off would hoy them out over the wall, we used to get them and pick all the good uns out, you'd be maybe running about with a six and a seven, or maybe a seven and a nine.[93]

Outerwear for Men

The men of Second and Third Class numbered 157 and 486 respectively, and in Third Class men outnumbered women by more than two to one. Due to a deadly combination of the women and children first convention, the lack of lifeboats, and unfamiliarity with the layout of the upper decks of the ship, they were the passengers least likely to survive the disaster (142 Second Class and 417 Third Class men perished in the sinking). The standard male attire of the period was dark wool three-piece suits, cotton shirts and flat caps. As discussed previously, the suits are likely to have been second-hand or, if bought new, ready-made. Poorer men only owned one suit and it was only discarded when worn out. Some men wore detachable collars with their shirts, along with ties, but others went collarless and tie-less every day except Sunday. For the men of Second Class, the ubiquitous lounge suit was also the garment of choice, although theirs were more likely to have been made-to-measure by a tailor or department store, and to be of better materials and more accurate in fit. Greater variety would also have been in evidence, in the form of different weights and shades or patterns of cloth, and possibly some variety in the colour of the waistcoat. Although the lounge suit amounted to a kind of uniform for virtually all men of the era, to contemporaries it was usually easy to tell what level of society different male passengers hailed from simply by the amount of wear, the fit, and the fabric quality of the suit. For the men of Second Class it would of course have been unthinkable to go out in public without collar and tie.

A vast gulf still existed between the different social groups of western European society, reinforced by the rigid divisions within the ship, and brutally demonstrated in the survival rates of the disaster. Clothing could and often did reinforce these social barriers, but just as many Third Class passengers on *Titanic* were seeking to escape the confines of a strict and seemingly unassailable class system, so their garments reflected their hopes and aspirations for a better life.

6. Dressed for Work: Crew and Servants

TITANIC SET OUT on her maiden voyage with a crew of almost 900, needed both to sail the ship and to look after the welfare of her very large number of passengers.[94] The crew was divided into three distinct categories: the Deck Department (70) carried out the navigation and steering of the vessel, and included the captain and his officers as well as the quartermasters, surgeons, seamen and lookouts. The Engine Department (327) was responsible for the machinery that propelled the ship, as well as the equipment for lighting, heating, ventilation and other electrically powered items. It included all the engineers as well as the firemen, trimmers, greasers and storekeepers. The Victualling Department (494) made up the largest group of crew members and was responsible for all aspects of passenger welfare. Many of these were stewards, but the galley section also included cooks of many different types such as a roast cook, a vegetable cook and a Hebrew cook. The staff of the à la carte restaurant were employed separately by the restaurant itself, and included further specialist cooks and waiters. The eight musicians were also separate from the main departments, as were the five post clerks and the two Marconi (telegraph) operators.

The captain and officers were in receipt of salaries from the White Star Line, but the remainder of the crew had to sign on for each voyage. There was some loyalty and continuity from one White Star Line trip to the next, but crew members could not automatically expect to be taken on for subsequent journeys, and the employment of trimmers, firemen and greasers, who were needed in large numbers, could vary considerably in steadiness. Around forty percent of the crew came from Hampshire (Southampton and its environs), but others hailed from all around Britain and Ireland. Many had followed the White Star Line express liner service to Southampton from Liverpool, where it had been based until 1907.

In his 1935 memoirs *Titanic and Other Ships*, Second Officer Charles Lightoller summed up the relationship between crew members and their ship: 'It is difficult to describe just where exactly that unity of feeling lies between a ship and her crew, but it is surely there in every ship that sails salt water. It is not always a feeling of affection either. A man can hate a ship worse than a human being.'[95]

Throughout the day and night crew members were dispersed all over the ship in the pursuit of their allotted duties. *Titanic* was new, and unusually vast, which took some getting used to. To those who had worked on *Titanic*'s sister ship, *Olympic*, the layout was familiar, but for others her size and complexity made it difficult to find one's way around. Able Seaman W. Lucas stated at the British Enquiry that it sometimes took him a long time to get from the crew accommodation to the decks: 'never knew my way...it was a new ship', while Charles Lightoller admitted that 'it took me fourteen days before I could find my way with confidence from one part of the ship to the other...a sailor does not walk about with a plan in his pocket, he must carry the ship in his head.'[96] Most of the crew's quarters (referred to as Glory Holes) were located on E Deck alongside, although separated from, passenger accommodation. They were situated close to a wide corridor and busy arterial route, nicknamed Scotland

Road after a main road in Liverpool. Many crew members slept on bunks in large dormitories, equipped with lockers for their possessions. Firemen and trimmers worked in shifts, and each watch of twenty-four men was allocated a separate dormitory. Men also had their own large washrooms, as they got so dirty during the course of their work. Senior staff members shared in smaller numbers, and were allotted more and better furniture, such as wooden bunks instead of iron ones, and wardrobes and tables. Deep sinks were provided in the wash rooms so that crew members could wash their clothing during the voyage and drying rooms were to be found next to the boiler casings.

The large number of staff was not unusual, especially aboard such a sizeable vessel, at a time when specialist equipment was only just beginning to make manual tasks of all kinds less labour-intensive. The White Star Line's special selling point was its lavish provision of services, so large numbers of crew were on hand to ensure that every aspect of a passenger's needs was catered for as smoothly and efficiently as possible.

In any case, the generous provision of staff on board ship reflected general practice in the wider world. In the years leading up to the First World War, a great number of people were still employed in domestic service. While the practice was soon to change, for the moment servants remained a part of normal life for the very wealthy. They also provided assistance to middle class families, and even to some working class homes. Passengers, particularly those in First Class, would have expected help with many aspects of their everyday lives on board ship, and some, as we have noted, brought their own personal servants with them. There were valets and personal maids, nursemaids and governesses. Indeed, the expectation that personal servants would be travelling with their employers meant that they were provided with their own separate dining saloon.

CREW UNIFORMS

Captain and Officers

The uniforms worn by officers of the White Star Line, and indeed other commercial shipping companies, were very similar to those of their counterparts in the Royal Navy. This deliberate association with a highly respected branch of the national establishment was intended to convey an impression of gravitas and authority. Seven of *Titanic*'s eight officers were also members of the Royal Naval Reserve, further strengthening the link between merchant officers and those of the Royal Navy. Sadly, definitive listings of requirements for White Star Line uniforms no longer exist, but it has been possible to piece together details of what was worn from photographs, surviving items, and a limited amount of documentation.

The firm that supplied uniforms for the crews of the White Star Line and other companies was Miller's Naval Tailors and Outfitters. It had branches in London and Tilbury, but the Southampton premises on the High Street and Canute Road produced many of the *Titanic* crew uniforms. The usual everyday uniform for officers, engineers and pursers was called service dress. It consisted of a cap with a black patent leather visor, a white shirt, black tie, dark, navy wool trousers and a dark navy wool undress jacket (commonly known as a monkey jacket). The jacket, which had lapels, was double breasted, with eight brass buttons, and finished just below hip level. The buttons were commissioned from several of different manufacturers, including the American firm Waterbury's, and Rayner and Sons of Liverpool.[97] They each featured an embossed White Star Line flag in the centre—the White Star Line emblem. The cap had an embroidered White Star Line cap badge stitched to the centre front. It had a red flag with a white star in the middle, surrounded by leaves in gold bullion thread, and surmounted by a crown. For formal

68 Replica of White Star Line cap badge as worn by *Titanic*'s crew members.

M: - S. 7. Sedunary (dec'd)   June   1912

MILLER & SONS,
TAILORS & OUTFITTERS,
4, & 6, Canute Road,
SOUTHAMPTON.

HIGH STREET, SOUTHAMPTON.
.. ST. FENCHURCH ST. LONDON, E.C.
.. ERT DOCKS & TILBURY DOCKS.

TELEGRAPHIC ADDRESSES,
MILLERSON, LONDON,
MILLERSON, SOUTHAMPTON.

TELEPHONE Nos HIGH STREET 57.   CANUTE ROAD 58.   LONDON, 6339, AVENUE.

No receipt valid unless given on our Printed Receipt form.

1911
Aug 31	4 Socks 4/-	Boots 7/11		11	11
	buttons 7	2 Shirts 5/10		6	5
	Pair Socks 4/-	Polish 4		1	4
Sept 19	Patrol Jacket			9	11
20	Collars 4/-	2 Shirts 6/10		6	10
	Coat			2	2 0
Oct 13	Suit			2	5 0
1912 Apl 10	buttons				7
				6	4 0
1911 Sept 19	C. Cash		10 0		
Dec 19	C. Cash		9 1		
	C. White Jacket		3 11		
1912 Jan 9	C. Cash		10 0		
Feby 28/12	u u		10 0	2 2 0
				£ 4 2 0

occasions, and when wearing the white Summer dress, caps also featured a removable white top. The captain's cap visor sported oak leaves made from gold bullion thread along the front edge. Just as in the Royal Navy, rank was also indicated by the inclusion of gold lace (or braid) stripes on the cuffs

69 Miller's bill to 2nd Third Class Steward Sidney Sedunary (dec'd) on the *Titanic*.

of the coat. The captain had four rows of lace, the top row with a loop. The chief officer had three rows with a loop at the top, and the first officer had two, again with a loop, whilst the second down to the sixth officer had a single stripe with a loop.[98] *Titanic's* engineers had a similar system of stripes, but without loops. For example, the chief engineer's cuffs included four straight stripes. The two telegraph operators also wore service dress, but since they were working for the Marconi Company, they had different cap badges. Theirs featured an 'M' in gold rather than the White Star Line flag.

Photographs of Captain Edward Smith on board ship, one of him together with four other officers, and another of *Titanic's* engineers, show them wearing the frock coat rather than the service dress jacket. The frock coat was more formal, and a natural choice for official photographs. Once again, this garment was very similar to that worn by officers of the Royal Navy. It was made from fine, dark, navy wool cloth, was double breasted, had ten brass buttons, and skirts that finished at mid-thigh level. Independent tailors were expected to produce uniforms for naval officers of all kinds, and there were guides to the correct styles and cutting methods involved. The Admiralty published details of all aspects of the uniforms of the Royal Navy in the Navy List, alongside an illustrated guide. They also produced specimen garments, which carried the Admiralty seal for authenticity. *The Cutter's*

71 Captain Edward J. Smith together with some of his officers, all of whom were lost. They are wearing frock coats and their caps have white tops.

70 (opposite) Officer's jacket from the White Star Line as worn by crew members on board *Titanic*.

Practical Guide provided tailors with a helpful synopsis of these regulations, and since the White Star Line frock coat was so similar to that worn by officers of the Royal Navy, it is worth quoting here:

> As regards the cutting of this coat…it is very much the same as an ordinary double-breasted frock. It is made from blue cloth, has an ordinary collar and turn, cut for six buttons, but only has five buttons on each breast and is made to button four; the width of lapel at fourth button to be 3 inches, tapering to 2 ½ at waist seam…The regulation length is 38 for an officer 5 feet 9 inches, varying ¼ inch for every inch of variation in height…The lining is of black silk.[99]

Not surprisingly, the Army and Navy Stores produced uniforms for members of the Royal Navy in their tailoring department, and their catalogues list individual items, fabrics and prices that would have been similar to those for Merchant Navy uniforms. Frock coats could be made in wool cloth of superfine or pilot varieties, while undress jackets were also available in cheaper serge. Gold lace could either be orris lace or the more costly wire lace. Dress trousers were made in superfine, and undress pairs in either blue doe, pilot or serge. The cost, in the 1907 catalogue, for best quality captain's frock coat and trousers were £5 13s 6d and £1 10s 6d respectively.[100] Regulation great coats of beaver or pilot wool were also produced, and officers of the *Titanic* would have worn similar versions as the ship entered the colder North Atlantic waters.

Under their frock coats or undress jackets officers wore wool cloth waistcoats of dark, navy blue over white cotton, or linen bib-front shirts, which buttoned down to chest level. As with the shirts worn by civilian men of the period, these had detachable stiff linen collars and cuffs, which were fixed in place with studs. The choice of a double collar, or a single one with folded corners (wings), seems to have been up to the individual, as both are seen in photographs. A narrow, black silk tie was knotted at the throat, and spotlessly shined black leather lace-up shoes were worn on the feet. For formal occasions, medals were pinned above the left breast, either full-size or abbreviated ribbon versions, and white gloves completed the ensemble.

We know that on the evening of Sunday 14 April Captain Smith attended a dinner in the à la carte restaurant given by Eleanor and George Widener, leading lights of American society. For this occasion an evening dress version of his uniform was necessary, and this was again based on equivalent items required for officers of the Royal Navy. Mess dress was the appropriate wear for formal dinners of this sort. It consisted of a short double breasted jacket, without tails, made from navy blue superfine wool. It extended to just above the hips and was worn open over a navy blue evening waistcoat. This was cut to reveal the stiff-fronted evening dress shirt with bow tie, and fastened with four buttons. Medals or smaller ribbon versions of decorations were worn above the left breast of the jacket and the relevant number of lace bands was stitched to the cuffs. Evening trousers of navy blue wool also featured gold lace braid along the side seams.

Able Seamen, Trimmers, Firemen and Greasers

There were twenty-nine able seamen on board *Titanic*. Their duties consisted of the basic deck-related tasks associated with the sailing and general maintenance of the ship, such as scrubbing the decks, and they were paid £5 per month plus board. Their uniform was a simple sailor suit, the equivalent of the Royal Navy ratings uniform, or 'square rig' consisting of a jumper or tunic of dark navy blue, which was pulled on over the head, and matching trousers. A flannel or shirt made from cotton, with a separate dark blue twill cotton sailor collar buttoned into place, was worn under the tunic.

72 Able seamen and other non-uniformed crew loading mail sacks onto *Titanic* at Queenstown.

The collar had three lines of white tape along the edge and a lanyard knotted around the neck. Beneath this a black silk neckerchief, folded into a loop and knotted at the front, was secured to the jumper with black tape. Head wear consisted of a tally cap, a traditional sailor's cap without a peak, with a black silk ribbon (tally).

The ship required a considerable amount of arduous manual labour to keep it moving through the water. This work was carried out by the trimmers (of which there were 73), firemen (175), who were sometimes called stokers, and the greasers (33). The normal work of the trimmers was to shovel the coal out of the bunkers and bring it to the boilers. The firemen loaded the coal into the boilers and made sure it was burning efficiently, while the greasers supervised the workings of the engines, lubricating them as required. It was dangerous and exhausting work.

In an article in the '*Titanic* Commutator' Fireman John Podesta wrote: 'It was the custom for we firemen and trimmers to go up on deck (at Queenstown) and carry the mails from the tender to the mail rooms'.[101] A surviving photograph of mail sacks being loaded onto the *Titanic* at Queenstown shows men in ordinary clothing of jackets, shirts, trousers and flat caps assisting other uniformed crewmen wearing pullovers with 'White Star Line' in white lettering, and these non-uniformed men may have been the firemen and trimmers mentioned by Podesta. As might be expected for men not normally seen by passengers, they would not have been required to wear uniforms. Their usual clothing was basic work wear, designed for the hard labour associated with the fuelling and maintenance of the massive reciprocating engines that powered the ship. It consisted of collarless cotton shirts, often with a neckerchief tied around the neck to soak up sweat and catch soot, and dark trousers of thick, sturdy cotton, sometimes with elasticized garters below the knees to keep the bottoms from picking up soot from the floor. Caps were worn, primarily to protect the head from excessive dirt. Alfred Fanstone, a Southampton resident, recalled the effect of such hard work on the body, and the ways in which these men filled their limited leisure time between voyages: 'All the people around Chapel, it was a rough fighting area because they used to come home from their voyages, which were "killer ships"; they all came home like walking skeletons, the stokers, and they had one glorious booze-up, which led to fighting and then off they went again.'[102]

There were 116 general stewards on board, as well as those with official job titles such as saloon, reception, deck and lounge stewards, bedroom stewards and bathroom stewards. Since these individuals were working mainly in public, they wore neat uniforms appropriate to their duties, designed to make them easily identifiable to passengers. Most male stewards wore dark wool trousers, white shirts, white cotton waistcoats and white cotton jackets. The waistcoat had four welted pockets (two above the breast and two above the hips), and was fastened with six brass White Star Line buttons. Over their waistcoats stewards wore white, single-breasted, waist-length jackets, with small lapels and short stand-up collars. These were again fastened with brass buttons, and had a pocket at the right breast. Some steward's roles required different uniforms: for example, deck stewards wore a dark navy wool suit with black bow tie, and a cap with a leather visor and a white star at the centre front.

The work of a steward was hectic, and often physically demanding. Chief Steward Hardy mentioned some of the duties of a bedroom steward to the U.S. Enquiry:

> Our duty does not take us on deck at all. We are entrusted with the passengers and that keeps us fully employed... each have a set of rooms to look after...a man has no more than twelve rooms...the way we work on board ship, all unnecessary lights are out at eleven, and then there are four bedroom stewards kept on from eleven to twelve... Then two bedroom stewards come along for the middle watch for twelve until four in the morning. Then they are relieved at half past five by all hands for the day. [103]

Jack Stagg, saloon steward, who did not live to testify at the inquiry, included the following account of the first day of the voyage in a letter to his wife:

what a day we have had of it, it's been nothing but work all day long, but I can tell you nothing as regards what people I have for nothing will be settled untill [*sic*] we leave Queenstown tomorrow, anyway we have only 317 first, and if I should be lucky enough to get a table at all it won't possibly be more than two that I shall have, still one must not grumble for there will be plenty without any.[104]

The tables Jack referred to are those in the dining saloons, where stewards were keen to serve, hopefully providing them with generous tips which were relied upon to supplement meagre wages. Jack added in a postscript to his letter that he had made 6d that day in tips.

There were seventeen stewardesses on board, and since women were not employed to wait on tables, their duties were confined to the cabin areas of the ship. Violet Jessop, stewardess in First Class, later wrote her memoirs. She described the work that she and her colleagues were required to undertake, which involved making beds, cleaning cabins and en suite bathrooms, vacuuming passageways, sweeping and dusting. They were also expected to bring breakfast and tea trays (or any other meals that might be requested), answer calls to do general errands, arrange flowers, turn down beds, put away clothes and look after the seasick.[105] Their clothing was similar to that worn by female domestic servants of the period: a simple functional and hard-wearing ankle-length dress, which was a dark colour and made from wool flannel or serge during the winter months. A stiff starched linen collar and cuffs, similar to those worn by men, was attached with studs, and a starched white linen cap pinned in place on the head. Stewardesses who had already worked on the liners for several years would recognize regular passengers. Violet Jessop knew Mr and Mrs Straus from previous trips, and Lucy, Lady Duff Gordon recalled her 'merry Irish stewardess with her soft Irish brogue and tales of timid ladies she had attended during hundreds of Atlantic crossings'.[106]

PERSONAL SERVANTS

Forty-three personal servants accompanied their employers on *Titanic*, some to assist on the voyage itself, but others just to continue their usual duties after arrival. Among the latter were two chauffeurs: Mr René Pernot, who worked for Benjamin Guggenheim, and George Swane, who served the Allison family. The Allisons also brought their personal cook,

Miss Amelia (known as Mildred) Brown. These individuals travelled Second Class, but the majority of personal servants travelled First Class in order to be on hand to run errands and carry out their usual tasks.

Personal Maids and Valets

Menservants travelling First Class with their masters included John Farthing, valet to Isador Straus, John Fry, valet to Bruce Ismay, and Victor Robbins, who attended John Astor. George Vanderbilt, who was due to sail on *Titanic* with his wife Edith, changed his mind at the last minute and sailed on *Olympic* instead. His valet, Fred Wheeler, consequently travelled Second Class on the *Titanic* with their luggage, and was lost. The manservant was expected to undertake all the duties associated with a gentleman's personal grooming, dressing and general well-being. Just as on land, during the voyage he laid out his master's clothing and accessories according to the time of day, assisted with dressing and undertook shaving and hair styling. The general maintenance of clothing such as washing, simple mending, pressing, brushing and shoe cleaning would also have been part of his duties. The employment of a valet was a sign of status and exclusivity, since only the head of a household or a wealthy younger man living alone would have one to himself. The valet was expected to be immaculately turned out, in a dark lounge suit, white shirt with stiff collar and cuffs and a tie. Similarly, no less than twenty of the ladies in First Class brought their lady's maids.

Valets and lady's maids were required to pack for their employers, and the convention that dictated several changes of clothes throughout the day meant that, even for short trips away this was an arduous and complicated process. As Cynthia Asquith points out, even for a short Friday to Monday country house visit, a large amount of clothing was needed: 'this necessitated at least one huge domed trunk, called a "Noah's Ark", an immense hat box and a heavy dressing-case. No one could grudge the perspiring porters the sixpences they seemed to think adequate reward for their Herculean labour'.[107] Rosina Harrison, personal maid to Lady Astor, recalled how, on a trip from London to New York, she was put in charge of twenty pieces of hand luggage, which were in addition to the many trunks that were stowed in the hold. She mentions the concerns she had about packing:

> Of course if she ever went away to visit I would accompany her and so it was that I learnt that very difficult art of packing. I say difficult, because by that I mean that while it's not hard to fill a case tidily, it is far from easy to pack it so that when you arrive at your destination you can take the things out in the same condition that you put them in—so that they are not creased, but ready to wear... Choosing what to take wasn't easy—mistresses before they leave are apt to be a bit hasty and short with you with their 'Oh, the usual things, you know what I like,' or 'I'll leave it to you Rose,' but when you get to the other end and you haven't brought what they want it's a very different story, and you are to blame. I soon learnt to be relentless in my questions to them.[108]

Items of luggage were very large and numerous by modern standards. Dress baskets were used, especially for garments to be kept in the cabin and accessed during the voyage. These were made from cane to reduce the weight, and covered with leather or canvas. Gamage's department store catalogue of 1914 includes a several examples. One of the largest was of compressed cane 'welted with leather with two locks and two trays'. It was 44 inches in length, 23½ inches in width and 26 inches deep. The weight before packing is listed as 50 lb, and the cost was 104 shillings. Some baskets included dividers to help separate different types of garments. Gamage's drawer cabin trunk, which opened

74 (opposite) Advertisements for luggage and dressing bags, *Illustrated London News*, 1911.

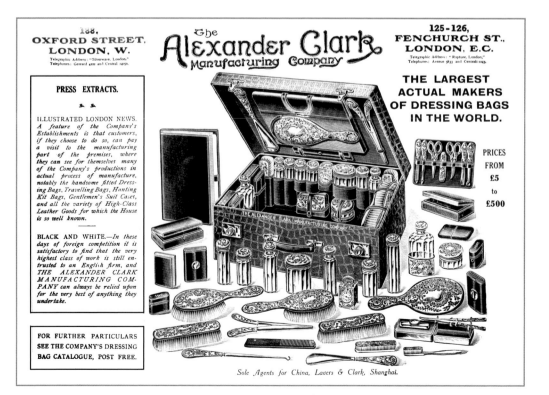

INNOVATION TRUNKS

PETIT CABIN WARDROBE TRUNK.

39 inches high; 21 inches wide;
13 inches deep
Exceptionally strong — will last
a lifetime.
Price £5 15 0

This size Innovation Trunk accommodates 5 to 8 dresses for a lady or 5 suits for a gentleman, with drawers giving ample accommodation for linen. No laborious packing or unpacking. No creased or wrinkled clothes on arrival at destination. Every article available immediately on opening the trunk.　**Price of Petit Trunk, £5 15 0**

WRITE FOR NEW CATALOGUE.

INNOVATION AGENCY
16 NEW BOND ST. LONDON, W.

PARIS. 10 Rue Auber.　　　　NEW YORK, 329 Fifth Avenue.

75 Advertisement for an 'Innovation' trunk, from a 1914 guidebook.

to reveal two large drawers, provided further assistance to maids and valets tasked with organizing their employers' belongings. Servants would also have worked with smaller dressing cases or fitted suit cases. These leather-covered pieces contained numerous brushes, silver-topped glass bottles, and implements for the care of the person such as manicure sets, and for men, shaving paraphernalia.

Sturdy trunks made from wood or steel were used for items to be stowed in the hold. Gamage's international oval trunk which was made of 'well seasoned wood foundation, covered strong brown canvas, good drop back lock, 2 strong clips, well protected with wood battens and strongly boned with strip iron, 2 leather handles, iron bottom underneath' was recommended as 'an ideal trunk for the Colonies'.[108] The Army and Navy Stores catalogue of 1907 also includes an enormous wardrobe trunk, in which garments could be suspended on hooks and hangers for easy access and minimal creasing. In addition to such trunks, numerous smaller cases and hat boxes would also have been necessary. The smartest groups of luggage were purchased as matching suites. Charlotte Drake Cardeza listed several

Louis Vuitton trunks as part of her insurance claim against the White Star Line, and this Paris firm was one of the most prestigious luggage producers. Founded in 1854, the firm launched its distinctive LV monogrammed canvas during the 1890s, and their flat-topped trunks and cases allowed for easy stacking.

Many of the tasks of a personal maid involved clothing. Rose Harrison stated that Lady Astor 'generally got through five sets of clothes in a day. This required from me a deal of organizing, pressing, cleaning and repairing'.[110] Maids were expected to carry out these duties, including the hand washing and drying of items, within their own quarters. In addition, their assistance was vital in the complicated process of dressing itself. In *The Edwardians*, a novel by Vita Sackville West, the character Viola describes her mother being dressed for dinner by her maid Button:

'I'm ready for you Button.' Button vanished into the dressing-room...Her mother was seated...while Button knelt before her, carefully drawing the silk stockings onto her feet and smoothing them nicely up the leg. Then her mother would rise, and, standing in her chemise, would allow the maid to fit the long stays of pink coutil, heavily boned, round her hips and slender figure, fastening the busk down the front, after many adjustments; then the suspenders would be clipped to the stockings; then the lacing would follow, beginning at the waist and travelling gradually up and down, until the necessary proportions had been achieved. The silk laces and their tags would fly out, under the maid's deft fingers, with the flick of a skilled worker mending a net. Then the pads of pink satin would be brought, and fastened into place on the hips and under the arms, still further to accentuate the smallness of the waist. Then the drawers; and then the petticoat would be spread into a ring on the floor, and Lucy would step into it on her high-heeled shoes, allowing Button to draw it up

76 Apron worn on board *Titanic* by Miss Francatelli, maid and secretary to Lady Duff Gordon.

and tie the tapes…Button I'm ready for my dress. Now be careful. Don't catch the hooks in my hair.

Button, gathering up the lovely mass of taffeta and tulle, held the bodice open while the Duchess flung off her wrap and dived gingerly into the billows of her dress…Button breathed a sigh of relief as she began doing up innumerable hooks at the back...'*There,* then,' said the Duchess, straightening herself...'I shall want you to wait up for me, Button, of course...My fan, Button! Good heavens, woman, what are you there for? One has to think of everything for oneself.' [111]

The smart, neat appearance of an employer was a matter of personal pride to a lady's maids, who were all too aware of how their abilities would be judged by potential future employers. Rather than wearing uniforms like other female domestic staff, personal maids were expected to dress in a sober yet up-to-date way. For example, ankle-length dresses might boast the new, straighter line, but would be in a muted, dark colour and made from an inexpensive fabric such as cotton or wool flannel. Although maids were frequently given the cast-off clothing of their employers, it was considered highly inappropriate to wear it in their presence, and showy, over-fashionable clothes were frowned upon. Aprons were worn during the execution of manual tasks such as washing and mending, and these were made from white cotton muslin and similar in style to children's pinafores. The bib section was wide, and extended in a broadening V-shape over the shoulders. The skirt covered that of the dress below, the two sides almost meeting at the back. Simple decoration such as white work embroidery embellished the bib, and sometimes extended down the centre front of the skirt. Miss Francatelli, secretary to Lady Duff Gordon, wore just such an apron during her escape from the *Titanic.*

All of the female servants who were travelling on board *Titanic* survived the disaster. The same cannot be said of their male counterparts, forty of whom were lost. Of the 899 predominantly male crew employed by the White Star Line, a massive 685 lost their lives. Many manned their posts to the last, bravely continuing to fulfil their allotted duties as the ship went down.

Notes

1 There are some discrepancies as to the exact numbers, but this and subsequent figures used (unless stated otherwise) are taken from the United States Senate Inquiry, which is published online at http://www.titanicinquiry.org.

2 A list of the clothes and accessories claimed for by Mrs Cardeza can be found in the appendix.

3 The figure for today's value is taken from the National Archives currency converter, online at http://www.nationalarchives.gov.uk/currency.

4 Maria Josefa Penasco (known as Pepita) had shopped at the Paris branch of Maison Lucile before setting out on *Titanic* (Judith B. Geller, *Titanic, Women and Children First* (Yeovil: Patrick Stevens, 1998), 60), while Charlotte Drake Cardeza claimed against the White Star Line for, among many other things, a rose gown and a white satin petticoat with lace and flowers, both by Madame Lucile and valued at $350 and $300 respectively.

5 Lucy, Lady Duff Gordon, *Discretions and Indiscretions* (London: 1932), 38.

6 Lucy, Lady Duff Gordon, *Discretions and Indiscretions* (London: 1932), 72–4.

7 Lucy, Lady Duff Gordon, *Discretions and Indiscretions* (London: 1932), 162–4.

8 Cynthia Asquith, *Remember and be Glad* (London: Barrie, 1952), quoted in Norah Waugh, *The Cut of Women's Clothes 1600–1930* (London: Faber, 1968), 295.

9 Letter from Mrs Ida Straus to Mrs Burbidge, National Maritime Museum LMQ/7/2/30.

10 Judith B. Geller, *Titanic, Women and Children First* (Yeovil: Patrick Stevens, 1998), 57. See also the appendix, this volume.

11 Lucy, Lady Duff Gordon, *Discretions and Indiscretions* (London: 1932), 42.

12 Elizabeth Ewing, *Dress and Undress, a history of women's underwear* (London: Bibliophile, 1978), 114–15.

13 Paul Poiret, *My First Fifty Years* (London: 1931).

14 M. Howarth, 'Holiday Raiment', *Every Woman's Encyclopaedia* No. 45, 5379, quoted in Katrina Rolley and Caroline Aish, *Fashion in Photographs 1900–20* (London: Batsford, 1992), 84.

15 Lucy, Lady Duff Gordon, *Discretions and Indiscretions* (London: 1932), 213.

16 Lucy, Lady Duff Gordon, *Discretions and Indiscretions* (London: 1932), 164.

17 Judith B. Geller, *Titanic, Women and Children First* (Yeovil: Patrick Stevens, 1998), 57.

18 Mrs Eric Pritchard, *The Cult of Chiffon* (London: 1902), quoted in Alison Gernsheim, *Fashion and Reality 1840–1914* (London: Faber & Faber, 1963), 86.

19 Alison Gernsheim, *Fashion and Reality 1840–1914* (London: Faber & Faber, 1963), 91.

20 Robert Farquarson, *The House of Commons from Within* (London: 1912), 212, quoted in Katrina Rolley and Caroline Aish, *Fashion in Photographs 1900–20* (London: Batsford, 1992), 52.

21 Diana Cooper, *The Rainbow Comes and Goes* (Salisbury: M. Russell, 1979), 96.

22 Harrods catalogue from c.1910–12, quoted in Katrina Rolley and Caroline Aish, *Fashion in Photographs 1900–20* (London: Batsford, 1992), 80.

23 John P. Eaton and Charles A. Haas, *Titanic: Triumph and Tragedy* (Yeovil: Patrick Stevens 1995), 283–5.

24 A riding habit of 1920, worn by Queen Maud of Norway, is illustrated and discussed in Anne Kjellberg and Susan North, *Style and Splendour: The Wardrobe of Queen Maud of Norway, 1896-1938* (London: V&A Publications, 2005), 66. Although the date is much later than 1912, the style is very similar to earlier examples. Queen Maude would have followed more traditional sartorial rules, especially when dressing for sporting activities.

25 Diana Cooper, *The Rainbow Comes and Goes* (Salisbury: M. Russell, 1979), 87.

26 Bruce Beveridge, *Titanic, The Ship Magnificent Vol. II* (Stroud: History Press, 2008), 287–8.

27 Gary Fisher and Dana McCauley, *Last Dinner on the Titanic* (London: Weidenfeld & Nicolson, 1997).

28 Bruce Beveridge, *Titanic, The Ship Magnificent Vol. II* (Stroud: History Press, 2008), 166 and 286–7.

29 Valerie D. Mendes and Amy de la Haye, *Fashion since 1900* (London: Thames & Hudson, 2010 2010), 17.

30 Claire Wilcox and Valerie Mendes, *Modern Fashion in Detail* (London: V&A Publications 1991), 92.

31 Lucy, Lady Duff Gordon, *Discretions and Indiscretions* (London: 1932), 38.

32 Lucy, Lady Duff Gordon, *Discretions and Indiscretions* (London: 1932), 74. The dress was called 'The Sighing Sound of Lips Unsatisfied'.

33 Judith B. Geller, *Titanic, Women and Children First* (Yeovil: Patrick Stevens, 1998), 83.

34 Judith B. Geller, *Titanic, Women and Children First* (Yeovil: Patrick Stevens, 1998), 66.

35 John Maxtone-Graham (ed.), *Titanic Survivor: The Memoirs of Violet Jessop, Stewardess* (Sutton, 1998), 211.

36 *The Dowagiac Daily News* (January 1912), quoted in Judith B. Geller, *Titanic, Women and Children First* (Yeovil: Patrick Stevens, 1998), 42–3.

37 John P. Eaton and Charles A. Haas, *Titanic: Triumph and Tragedy* (Yeovil: Patrick Stevens 1995), 283–5.

38 Lucy, Lady Duff Gordon, *Discretions and Indiscretions* (London: 1932), 175.

39 Judith B. Geller, *Titanic, Women and Children First* (Yeovil: Patrick Stevens, 1998), 76.

40 Cynthia Asquith, *Remember and be Glad* (London: Barrie, 1952), 173.

41 Bruce Beveridge, *Titanic, The Ship Magnificent Vol. II* (Stroud: History Press, 2008), 251.

42 Sally Kevill-Davies, *Yesterday's Children: The Antiques and History of Childcare* (Woodbridge: Antique Collectors' Club, 1991), 175.

43 Philip Warren, *Foundations of Fashion, the Symington Corsetry Collection 1860 – 1990* (Leicestershire County Council, Museums, Arts and Records Service, 2001), 75.

44 Jonathan Gathorne-Hardy, *The Rise and Fall of the British Nanny* (London: London : Weidenfeld & Nicholson, 1993), 172.

45 *Yesterday's Shopping, Gamages General Catalogue, 1914* (Ware: Wordsworth Editions Ltd, 1994).

46 Names, ages and type of ticket have been taken from the passenger lists published at http://www.encyclopedia-titanica.org/titanic_passenger_list/.

47 Quoted in Donald Hyslop, Alastair Forsyth and Sheila Jemima, *Titanic Voices: Memories from the Fateful Voyage* (Sutton Publishing, 1997), 120–1.

48 Katharine Moore, *Queen Victoria is Very Ill* (London: Allison & Busby, 1988), 34.

49 Compton Mackenzie, *My Life and Times, Octaves 1 and 2* (London: Chatto & Windus, 1963–4), quoted in Elizabeth Ewing, *History of Children's Costume* (London: Bibliophile, 1977), 92.

50 Mary Keen, quoted in Max Arthur (ed.), *Lost Voices of the Edwardians* (London: Harper, 2006), 19.

51 Harrods advertisement from *The Queen, The Lady's Newspaper* (March 30, 1912), 5.

52 Biographies of many of the passengers on board *Titanic* are published online at http://www.encyclopedia-titanica.org.

53 Francis Davis Millet, excerpt from letter written on board *Titanic* on Thursday, 11 April 1912. Worcestershire Record Office: BA 11302 X705:1235.

54 'Fashionable Evening Clothes', *The Sartorial Art Journal* (New York: Jno. J. Mitchell Co.), Vol. XXXVIII, No. 5, November 1912, 211.

55 V. Sackville-West, *The Edwardians* (London: The Hogarth Press, 1960), 168.

56 R. H. Langbridge (ed.), *Edwardian Shopping, A selection from the Army & Navy Stores Catalogues, 1898–1913* (David & Charles, 1975).

57 *The Sartorial Art Journal* (New York: Jno. J. Mitchell Co.), Vol. XXXVIII, No. 5, November 1912, 231.

58 'Sturgis Survivors Tell Experiences', *The Sturgis Times Democrat* (22 April 1912), quoted in Judith B. Geller, *Titanic, Women and Children First* (Yeovil: Patrick Stevens, 1998), 43.

59 Juliet Nicholson, *The Perfect Summer, Dancing into Shadow in 1911* (London: John Murray, 2006), 31.

60 *The Sartorial Art Journal* (New York: Jno. J. Mitchell Co.), Vol. XXXVIII, No. 5, November 1912, 219.

61 The 'Major' of Today, *Clothes and the Man. Hints on The Wearing and Caring of Clothes* (London: Grant Richards, 1900), 123, quoted in Katrina Rolley and Caroline Aish, *Fashion in Photographs 1900–20* (London: Batsford, 1992), 23.

62 R. H. Langbridge (ed.), *Edwardian Shopping, A selection from the Army & Navy Stores Catalogues, 1898–1913* (David & Charles, 1975).

63 Most of these facilities are listed enthusiastically by Francis Millet in a letter written aboard *Titanic* on Thursday, 11 April 1912. Worcestershire Record Office: BA 11302 X705:1235.

64 Bruce Beveridge, *Titanic, The Ship Magnificent Vol. II* (Stroud: History Press, 2008), 204–12.

65 'Accessories for Evening Dress' *The Sartorial Art Journal* (New York: Jno. J. Mitchell Co.), Vol. XXXVIII, No. 5, November 1912, 211.

66 The 'Major' of Today, *Clothes and the Man. The Wearing and Caring of Clothes* (Grant Richards, 1900), 145, quoted in Katrina Rolley and Caroline Aish, *Fashion in Photographs 1900–20* (London: Batsford, 1992), 46.

67 Letter from Francis Davis Millet written on board *Titanic* on Thursday, 11 April 1912. Worcestershire Record Office: BA 11302 X705:1235.

68 Agreement and Account of Crew (PRO London: BT100/259), United States Senate (62nd Congress), Subcommittee Hearings of the Committee on Commerce, *Titanic* Disaster, Washington 1912.

69 http://www.encyclopedia-titanica.org/titanic-biography/reginald-charles-coleridge.html.

70 Judith B. Geller, *Titanic, Women and Children First* (Yeovil: Patrick Stevens, 1998), 115.

71 Nick Barratt, *Lost Voices from the Titanic : the Definitive Oral History* (London: Preface, 2009), 96.

72 Judith B. Geller, *Titanic, Women and Children First* (Yeovil: Patrick Stevens, 1998), 124.

73 Quoted in Donald Hyslop, Alastair Forsyth and Sheila Jemima, *Titanic Voices: Memories from the Fateful Voyage* (Sutton Publishing, 1997), 125.

74 Second Class dinner menu, RMS *Titanic*, 14 April 1912, Walter Lord Collection, National Maritime Museum F5425.

75 'U.S. Immigration Statistics: Immigration Station at Ellis Island, NY', published at http://www.nps.gov/elis/forteachers/upload/Statistics.pdf.

76 'Immigrants admitted to Canada by Ethnic Origin 1896-1915' (Statistics Section – Department of Citizenship and Immigration Canada), published at http://www.theshipslist.com/Forms/canadastats.htm.

77 'The Demographics of *Titanic* passengers: Breakdown of passengers by nationality', published at http://www.ithaca.edu/staff/jhenderson/titanic.html.

78 Judith B. Geller, *Titanic, Women and Children First* (Yeovil: Patrick Stevens, 1998), 137–94.

79 *Record of Bodies and Effects (Passengers and Crew S.S. 'Titanic') Recovered by Cable Steamer 'MacKay Bennett' Including Bodies Buried at Sea and Bodies Delivered at Morgue in Halifax*, N.S. Public Archives of Nova Scotia, Halifax, N.S., Manuscript Group 100, Vol. 229, No. 3d, Accession 1976-191, 76. Published at http://www.encyclopedia-titanica.org/victims.php.

80 Gertrude Jekyll, *Old West Surrey, Some Notes and Memories* (London: 1904), 262–4.

81 Judith B. Geller, *Titanic, Women and Children First* (Yeovil: Patrick Stevens, 1998).

82 *Liverpool Review* (1884), quoted in Anne Brogden, 'Paddy's Market', *Costume* (Vol. 38, 2004), 110.

83 Lena Burton, in Max Arthur (ed.), *Lost Voices of the Edwardians* (London: Harper, 2006), 35.

84 Anne Taylor, in Max Arthur (ed.), *Lost Voices of the Edwardians* (London: Harper, 2006), 14.

85 Body no. 13, Record of Bodies and Effects, published at http://www.encyclopedia-titanica.org/victims.php.

86 Body no. 8, Record of Bodies and Effects published at http://www.encyclopedia-titanica.org/victims.php.

87 Cynthia Asquith, *Remember and Be Glad* (London: 1952), 76.

88 Judith B. Geller, *Titanic, Women and Children First* (Yeovil: Patrick Stevens, 1998), 99–102.

89 Cynthia Asquith, *Remember and be Glad* (London: 1952), 57.

90 Annie Swain, in Max Arthur (ed.), *Lost Voices of the Edwardians* (London: Harper, 2006), 220–1.

91 Max Arthur (ed.), *Lost Voices of the Edwardians* (London: Harper, 2006), 42.

92 Judith B. Geller, *Titanic, Women and Children First* (Yeovil: Patrick Stevens, 1998), 139.

93 Reece Elliott, in Max Arthur (ed.), *Lost Voices of the Edwardians* (London: Harper, 2006), 16.

94 According to the United States Senate Enquiry, 899 crew members were present on board. Statistics for specific groups within the main departments are taken from the crew list published in Bruce Beveridge, *Titanic, The Ship Magnificent Vol. II* (Stroud: History Press, 2008), 460–2.

95 C. Lightoller, quoted in Donald Hyslop, Alastair Forsyth and Sheila Jemima, *Titanic Voices: Memories from the Fateful Voyage* (Sutton Publishing, 1997), 92.

96 Donald Hyslop, Alastair Forsyth and Sheila Jemima, *Titanic Voices: Memories from the Fateful Voyage* (Sutton Publishing, 1997), 91.

97 http://www.titanicitems.com/button.htm.

98 John Hemmert, 'White Star Line Officer's Uniform Circa 1912', published at http://www.encyclopedia-titanica.org/white-star-line-uniform-1912.html.

99 W. D. F. Vincent, *The Cutter's Practical Guide to the Cutting of all kinds of Garments made by Tailors for Gentlemen by Model Patterns* (London: John Williamson, 1904), 86.

100 *Yesterday's Shopping, The Army & Navy Stores Catalogue 1907* (David and Charles, 1969), 863.

101 Quoted in Donald Hyslop, Alastair Forsyth and Sheila Jemima, *Titanic Voices: Memories from the Fateful Voyage* (Sutton Publishing, 1997), 81.

102 Alfred Fanstone (Southampton City Heritage Oral History), quoted in Hyslop, Donald, Forsyth, Alastair and Jemima, Sheila, *Titanic Voices* (Southampton, 2006), 62.

103 Chief Steward Hardy's evidence to the U.S. Enquiry, quoted in Donald Hyslop, Alastair Forsyth and Sheila Jemima, *Titanic Voices: Memories from the Fateful Voyage* (Sutton Publishing, 1997), 80–1.

104 Letter from Saloon Steward Jack Stagg to his wife (Southampton City Heritage Collections), quoted in Donald Hyslop, Alastair Forsyth and Sheila Jemima, *Titanic Voices: Memories from the Fateful Voyage* (Sutton Publishing, 1997), 128.

105 John Maxtone-Graham (ed.), *Titanic Survivor: The Memoirs of Violet Jessop, Stewardess* (Sutton, 1998), 18.

106 Lucy, Lady Duff Gordon, *Discretions and Indiscretions* (London: 1932), 164.

107 Cynthia Asquith, *Remember and Be Glad* (London: 1952), 166.

108 Rosina Harrison, *Rose: My Life in Service* (London: Cassell, 1976), 21.

109 *Yesterday's Shopping, Gamages General Catalogue, 1914* (Ware: Wordsworth Editions Ltd, 1994), 112–13.

110 Rosina Harrison, *Rose: My Life in Service* (London: Cassell, 1976), 64.

111 V. Sackville-West, *The Edwardians* (London: The Hogarth Press, 1960), 39–43.

Appendix: Compensation Claims

Survivors of the sinking of the *Titanic* filed claims in the U.S. courts against the White Star Line for compensation for loss of life and property. The archival papers relating to these claims are now held by the U.S. National Archives and Records Administration. Details of three of the claims, of particular interest because of the items of clothing listed, are given here.

Mrs Charlotte Cardeza listed in detail the extensive wardrobe she had acquired on her travels around European capitals. The items claimed for by another First Class passenger, Mrs Margaret 'Molly' Brown, were fewer but still included some very expensive items. Both provide a contrast with the claim of Second Class passenger, Mrs Allen Becker, who was travelling with her three children, Ruth, aged 12, Marion, aged 4, and Richard, aged 1. The most expensive single item of clothing she claimed for was her suit of tan silk ($30), while eight of Mrs Cardeza's eleven suits cost over $200 each.

All figures given below are the amounts in U.S. dollars as recorded in the claims.

MRS CHARLOTTE CARDEZA

INNOVATION TRUNK	$75
Blue Russian dress	275
Black chiffon dress, with white dots, trimmed with cerise, Princess	215
White chiffon dress, with black dots and flowers, Redfern, Paris	270
White dress, with gray stripe and gray embroidery and lace, Lord & Taylor	155
White chiffon dress, with pink roses and black ribbon border, Redfern, Paris	340
Mauve crepe brocade dress, Redfern, Paris	300
Coral pink chiffon dress, trimmed with embroidery and lace, Lord & Taylor	352
White broadcloth dress, with Venetian lace, Redfern, Paris	500
Mulberry velvet dress, Ungar, Vienna	345
Black Chiffon and velvet dress, Ungar, Vienna	287
Baby blue dotted lawn dress, with lace, Lord & Taylor	150
White chiffon dress, with blue flowers, Redfern, Paris	415
Navy china dress, with polka dots, covered with chiffon, Lord & Taylor	150
Pink flannel wrapper, Paris	50

INNOVATION TRUNK	75
Cream corded silk dress, covered with chiffon and gold lace, Paris	500
White brocade chiffon tunic, silver trimmings, Ungar, Vienna	390
Iridescent spangled net dress, Redfern, Paris	480

Green and black lace dress, Worth, Paris 800
Bright pink with Venetian lace, waist,
Lord & Taylor 300
Pale pink satin skirt, pale blue tunic with silver,
Lord & Taylor 295
Salmon pink with gold dress, Ungar, Vienna 300
White and silver brocade, pink roses,
Lord & Taylor 225
Rose gown, Lucille [sic] 350
Blue satin with cerise gown, Lord & Taylor 255
Black net shower of rice gown, Lord & Taylor 255
White satin petticoat, Rouff, Paris 75

LOUIS VUITTON, TRAY TRUNK 80
Pink evening coat, trimmed with silver, Irish lace,
Redfern, Paris 380
Green taffeta jacket, embroidered with pink roses,
Redfern, Paris 100
Blue satin embroidered jacket 110
White satin coat, trimmed with lace,
Lord & Taylor 155
Real lace gamp. Applique, Redfern, Paris 195
Real lace gamp. Brussels, Redfern, Paris 155
Real lace gamp. Milanese, Redfern, Paris 120
Lace gamp. Applique 180
White satin petticoat, lace and flowers,
Lucille [sic], London 200
White flannel petticoat, lace and silk ruffles 55
Pink flannel petticoat, lace and silk ruffles 75
Blue Jersey petticoat, Lord & Taylor 75
Rose Jersey petticoat, Lord & Taylor 60
White Jersey petticoat, Lord & Taylor 60
White Jersey petticoat, lace chiffon, and roses,
Lord & Taylor 95
White Jersey petticoat, shoestring ruffles,
Lord & Taylor 65
White satin slip, Lord & Taylor 45
White net dress, embroidery and lace, pink ribbon
hobble, Lord & Taylor 400
White net dress, black polka dots, lined with green
chiffon, Lord & Taylor 100
Pink satin slip, Derocher, Paris 40
White lawn negligee with lace and pink ribbons.
Derocher, Paris 195
Pink brocade dressing jacket and skirt with lace
ruffles, Rouff, Paris 182
Pink chiffon skirt, with Greek, Irish and Val lace
with dressing saque, Rouff, Paris. 250
Pink satin dressing saque, with lace. New York 120

Blue tea gown, satin and embroidery.
Ungar, Vienna 160
Pink wrapper, with fillet lace collar, Rouff, Paris 78
Pink pongee wrapper, Rouff, Paris 52
Heavy linen skirt, embroidered roleschilo lace.
Florence 250
Heavy linen skirt, embroidered and fillet lace.
Florence 240
Heavy linen skirt, Florence
Carlsbad, Hungary 300
Fine embroidered linen and val. lace dress.
Redfern, Paris. 410
Satin lining for skirt, Redfern, Paris 39
Fine embroidered and val. Lace princess.
Carlsbad 350
Fine embroidered and Irish lace dress, Lillie 270
Heavy embroidered waist, fillet lace 75
Heavy embroidered waist, carved embroidery 62
Heavy embroidered waist 58
Fine embroidered and waist lace. New York 110

VUITTON TRUNK 80
Fine embroidered and lace waist. New York 110
Fine embroidered and Irish lace waist, small
blocks. Redfern, Paris 90
Fine embroidered forget-me-nots and
Irish waist. Zigzag. 125
Fine embroidered waist, chrysanthemums and
narrow lace 80
Fine embroidered waist, roses and fillet lace 105
Fine embroidered waist, val lace. Carlsbad 100
Fine embroidered waist, Irish lace. Carslbad 92
Fine embroidered waist, lace. Ungar, Vienna 75
Fine embroidered waist, fillet lace. Florence 100
Irish lace and English embroidery princess gown.
Lord & Taylor 235
Net embroidery and Venetian lace waist 400
Fillet and Venetian lace waist. Paris 485
2 cambric petticoats, Hamburg edging 42
Cambric petticoat, hand embroidered and lace,
white ribbons. Redfern, Paris 90
Cambric petticoat, hand embroidered and lace,
pink ribbons. Redfern, Paris 97

MENDEL TRUNK 90
Vest for tailor made coats 25
Chiffon waist, val lace. Redfern, Paris 445
Lace waist. Ungar, Vienna 80
Gold under chiffon waist. Redfern, Paris 90

Dark blue satin waist, lace yoke. Redfern, Paris 95
Pink chiffon dressing saque, with Greek, Irish
    and Val. Lace. 182
Dark blue chiffon lace waist, lace yoke. Ungar, Vienna
    65
Chiffon waist for brown tailor-made dress.
    Lord & Taylor 75
Chiffon waist for Zibeline tailor-made. Ungar, Vienna
    70
Rose waist for Rose tailor-made. Ungar, Vienna 60
French, Irish lace waist 100
Irish lace waist. London 135
White china silk waist. Carlsbad lace 65

MENDEL
Dark navy blue suit. Ungar. Vienna 105
Rose serge suit, Norfolk style. Ungar, Vienna 95
Zibeling suit. Vienna 100
Brown satin suit. Lord & Taylor 275
Black Brocade suit, samphire blue velvet. Ungar,
    Vienna 354
Pongee coat and skirt, trimmed with brown.
    Paris 100
Pink silk shoulder scarf with white marabou
    edging. Lord & Taylor 55
One pair pads covered with ribbon and new
    cover for pads 3.5
Rose skirt ribbon 9.75

No. 1 Drawer of Mendel
14 pairs auto gloves, leather 1 wool 37
20 pairs new white kid gloves, 16 long, 4 short 65
3 pairs new black kid gloves, short 10.5
30 pairs new white silk gloves 16 long, 14 short 72
1 pair black silk gloves, short 2.25
3 pairs navy silk gloves, long 8.25
10 pairs, white kid gloves, long 35
3 pairs white kid gloves, short 7.5

No. 2 Drawer of Mendel
3 wisks 1.25
Package needles, pins, cotton, silk and
    sewing things 5
Pieces of lace for waist, also box of belts 700
Sewing box, pair pink garters, pair white garters 14
Pink ribbon, new rushes, rose and white, collar bones,
    ribbons for slippers 10
Package of fancy ribbons (McCreedy) 25
Beads for blue satin with ermine 2

Tape measure, ribbons for night gown 2.75
Irish pin cushion 8
Pink and white silk braid for underwear.
    London 4.85

No. 3 Drawer of Mendel
2 transformations 200
Box with flowers for hair 32
Box with combs for hair 125
Box of set combs for hair. Wanamaker's 18
2 cakes Vera Violette soap 2
1 cake soap Grasse 1.75
Manicure set and nail buffer 9.25
Box with green velvet ribbon for hair 15
1 Ivory comb 10
Fillet lace jabot and yoke 35
Net jabot with Irish lace 16
Embroidered linen jabot with Irish lace 48
Irish lace jabot 21.5
Val. lace jabot. Carlsbad 24
Bohemian lace jabot 12
Antique beaded purse. Vienna 98
Blue velvet ribbon for hair 4
Carlsbad pin cushion 25
Hair pins, safety pins, gold, and toilet
    articles 100
2 lace scarfs 90
1 piece albatross 15
1 piece pink brocade 8.5

No. 4 Drawer of Mendel
Music box, little bird 350
Leather picture frame 25
Mother-of-pearl and lace fan 250
Large beaded bag 126
Small beaded purse 72
Opera glasses 125
2 mosaic frames 20
2 silver frames 50
2 silver and gilt frames 64

VUITTON DRESS TRUNK 80
12 handkerchiefs, Hutchinson, N.Y. (6 with
    Mechlin lace edge, 6 with Val. lace edge) 36
12 fine real lace handkerchiefs with monogram 48
11 fine handkerchiefs with coat-of-arms. Wixler,
    Zurich 67
6 fine double hemstitched handkerchiefs with
    Cardeza 35

1 fine glove handkerchief, Mechlin lace,
embroidered monogram 8

1 fine glove handkerchief, Pont de Paris lace 10

2 Florence lace sachet sacks or bags 15

1 Glove fine linen handkerchief embroidered Cardeza
5

Pink dressing sack. Vienna 8.8

1 Singlet swan, light weight. Altman & Co. 1.18

1 Singlet swan, light weight. Saka & Co. 1.25

2 Singlets swan, light weight, tag 118 2.36

5 Singlets swan, light weight, Wanamakers 6.5

2 Singlet Star, light weight 3

2 Singlet swan, light weight, low neck 2

2 pair medium weight wool tights 13

2 pair white silk knickers. London 15

1 pair pink silk knickers. London 8

2 pair pink silk tights. Bon Marche, Paris 14

2 pair pink silk underwaists. Bon Marche, Paris 8

2 pair pink silk Singlet with crochet 6

1 pair pink silk drawers. New York 4.58

1 pair white silk drawers. New York 4.58

4 blue flannel nightgowns 20

White and blue jacket 12

White Shetland wool auto scarf. Vienna 8

3 camel's hair knit jackets, heavy. Paris 12

17 pair black silk stockings embroidered
and lace 150

4 pair black wool stockings 16

4 pair fancy colour silk stockings 20

4 pair white silk stockings 20

2 pair white cotton stockings 3

4 pair pink wool stockings 16

2 pink silk chemises 35

3 pairs silk drawers 47

2 pairs chimaloons 16

bed wrap 27

4 pairs drawers, lace and embroidery 85

1 embroidered chemise 9

Night gown, English style, wreath and bees.
Rouff, Paris 35

Combination, Empire style, wreath and bees.
Rouff, Paris 28

1 pair drawers, wreath and bees. Rouff, Paris 19

1 pair drawers, butterflies and wreaths.
Rouff, Paris 24

1 corset cover, butterflies and wreaths,
antique lace. Rouff, Paris 21

2 combinations and drawers to match. English
embroidery. Rouff, Paris 50

2 corset covers and drawers to match. English
embroidery. Rouff, Paris 18

2 white china silk underwaists. Rouff, Paris 16.8

1 white china silk underwaist. Rouff, Paris 8.4

1 White satin waist, covered with chiffon.
Redfern, Paris 30

2 White satin waists. Low neck 50

2 pink underwaists. Lord & Taylor 46

1 White satin gamp. Lord & Taylor 18

1 Pink satin gamp. Lord & Taylor 18

1 White satin, short sleeves underwaist,
covered with chiffon. 25

1 White satin low neck underwaist.
Ungar, Vienna 20

2 Pink china silk underwaists. Ungar, Vienna 42

Fel Toir curtain. Wixler, Zurich 600

3 heavy Lourve silk nightgowns. 75

2 Pink silk nightgowns. Rouff, Paris 40

3 Pink silk nightgowns. New York 75

3 Pink thin silk nightgowns 66

1 Brusse silk nightgown 30

2 lace bureau scarfs. Rouff, Paris 420

Long near seal coat trimmed with ermine.
Dresden 800

Long ermine coat. New York 1,400

Chinchilla coat, Irish lace. New York 6,000

Chinchilla stole. Ungar, Carlsbad 1,400

Silver fox stole. New York 2,350

Ermine stole Muff. Dresden 180

Fur gloves for auto 3

Long white moth bag for ermine coat 1.5

1 Pink Paradise 75

1 Elephant's breath Paradise 80

2 Pink Paradise 125

1 Black aigrette 100

1 Light blue aigrette 80

Small breast of Paradise 20

White ostrich feather, 20" long 35

Bunch of 13 white feathers 42

Long grey and white ostrich feather 50

5 white ostrich feathers 120

2 purple ostrich feathers 33

2 natural ostrich feathers 50

7 Black ostrich feathers 130

1 black ostrich feather, extra long 35

7 Omdurman ostrich feathers 35

2 large white ostrich feathers 70

1 large white aigrette 200

1 blue ostrich feather 25

LOUIS VUITTON HAT TRUNK	60
7 black veils	11
1 black lace veil	8
3 black and white veils	4
1 blue lace veil	8
1 blue lace veil	5.5
3 coloured veils	6
6 coloured scarfs	72
5 auto veils	50
5 scarfs	55
2 silk and lace theatre caps. Lord & Taylor	25.75
White and coral hair band. Lord & Taylor	23.5
Pink band, gold tassel. Lord & Taylor	17.9
2 pink roses	5
Blue hat, feather band and paradise. Valette, Paris	54
Bordeaux velvet hat, very long ostrich feather. Valette, Paris	85
Black velvet hat, chinchilla band and Paradise. Valette, Paris.	150
Velvet hat with ermine. New York	85
Seal hat with ermine. Dresden	40
Light blue velvet hat with pink roses. Valette, Paris	50
22 hat pins	86
6 gold hat pins	270
9 Assorted hat pins	139
9 Bar pins	500

LOUIS VUITTON HAT TRUNK	60
Large black straw hat, yellow Paradise. Valette, Paris	76
Light green velvet hat, black and green ostrich feathers. Valette, Paris	80
Large black velvet hat, black ostrich plume. Lord & Taylor	55
Mauve hat, ostrich feathers. Valette, Paris	70
Champagne straw hat, pink ostrich feathers. Valette, Paris	75
White linen parasol, Swiss embroidery. Lucerne	18
White taffeta silk parasol, hand painted, porcelain handle. Lord & Taylor	60
Red taffeta silk parasol. Vienna	35
White applique lace parasol. Redfern, Paris	300
2 Yeager [sic] wool caps for hunting	3
1 pair wool stockings for hunting	2
1 pair corsets. Redfern, Paris	35
2 Girdles. Paris	24
2 pair garter suspenders, 2 white silk laces, Tissue paper	8

LOUIS VUITTON SHOE TRUNK	100
1 pair satin slippers, gilt rhinestone buckles	16
1 pair kid slippers	7
1 pair blue kid slippers, stockings to match	10
1 pair light blue satin slippers, stockings to match. Paris	18
1 pair blue satin slippers.	18
1 pair rose satin slippers. Paris	16
1 pair white kid slippers, silk and wool stockings	12
1 pair covert cloth gaiters	8
1 pair white canvas gaiters	6
1 pair black velvet gaiters	12
1 pair long gaiters	14
Package shoe laces, ribbons, etc. for shoes and slippers	4
1 pair new white kid slippers, large gilt buckles	5
1 pair, new white kid slippers, enamel buckles	9
1 pair, new white kid slippers	8
1 pair black satin slippers, rhinestone buckles and silk stockings	21
1 pair black satin slippers, roses	16
1 pair purple satin slippers and stockings to match green slippers	18
1 pair red felt bedroom slippers, fur tops	6
1 pair pink satin slippers, quilted. Paris	9
1 pair pink satin bedroom slippers, white fur	12
11 pairs of shoes and 1 pair patent leather laced, heavy soles	120

INNOVATION STEAMER TRUNK	40
White jersey petticoat. Redfern, Paris	72
4 lace and embroidered pillow cases. Rouff, Paris	119
Pink satin pillow slip. Rouff, Paris	29
White silk knitted scarf, heavy fringe. London	35
2 silk nightgowns. Rouff, Paris	60
Embroidered chemise and drawers.	30
2 pairs silk stockings, white feet	8
1 pair black wool stockings	8
2 pink satin underwaists. Ungar and Redfern, Paris	45
Pink satin gamp. Lord & Taylor	15
2 china silk underwaists	16.8
1 Pink silk ribbed undervest	4
2 singlets	3.75
1 flannel skirt and cambric hair jacket	19
5 auto veils	25
6 pairs white silk gloves	15
1 pair gray suede gloves	2

Blue serge waist. Lord & Taylor	90
Light blue dress, trimmed with silver. Ungar, Vienna	340
White satin dress, applique lace. Lord & Taylor	350
Blue taffeta dress. Samase yoke. Lord & Taylor	200
White camel's hair coat. Redfern, Paris	210
Blue serge suit, trimmed with old rose. Lord & Taylor	200
Gray suit trimmed with Irish lace. Lord & Taylor	210
Blue flowered wrapper. Vienna	50
Gray squirrel fur coat	200

DRESS SUIT CASE — 500

Pink silk nightgown and dressing saque	36
Brushes, combs and toilet articles, about	50

GOYARD TRAY TRUNK — 58

White embroidered dress, Paris	70
Blue polka dot dress, Paris	126
Blue lace evening dress. Paris	250
Embroidered bird dress. Paris	225
Veils. Paris	100
Gloves, Paris	200
Underwear, Paris	400
Hat pins, Paris	100
Blue silk dress, Berlin	240
Lace waist, Berlin	80
Lace gown, Berlin	300
Tailor suit. Berlin	200
Hat, Berlin	75
White Baby lamb coat. Russia	1,500
Mink stole and muff. Russia	800
Mole skin muff and coat. Paris	400
Tailor suit. Paris	223
Blue and silver dress. Paris	375
Tailor suit, trimmed ermine. Paris	300
Blue silk coat and skirt. Irish lace. Paris	250
Evening dress. Paris	275
Evening coat. Paris	200
Tailor suit. Paris	225
Hat trunk	60
Hats, Paris	742

MRS MARGARET BROWN

Street furs	$300
Ermine Collarette	75
Ermine opera Cape	500

Brussels Lace Gown	375
Persian Over dress	175
6 Dinner Gowns ($75 each)	450
Green Lace Gown	175
1 Sealskin Jacket	700
4 Gowns ($200 each)	800
1 necklace	20,000
Odd laces	200
1 Pearl Brooch	150
14 hats	225
6 lace shirt waists	175
6 Embroidered waists, lace	140
Silk hosiery	75
Lingerie	300
2 Japanese Kimonos	50
1 Black Satin Gown	150
1 blue and white serge gown	75
3 satin evening gowns	450
1 Irish Lace gown	150
3 dozen gloves	50
1 hat	35
6 shoes (10 Each)	60
4 tailored gowns and 2 coats	500
3 shoes	36
1 evening wrap	150
4 Evening slippers	16
Brown velvet gown	200
Brown velvet coat	100
2 black gowns	180

MRS ALLEN BECKER

1 hat	$4
1 hat, linen	2
1 Tan silk suit	30
1 silk dress	18
1 Silk dress	12
Mohair dress	10
1 Serge suit	25
1 Gray cloth skirt	5
1 Black cloth skirt	5
7 White shirt waists	21
1 White mohair shirt	7
1 Black silk shirt waist	3
1 Blue messaline silk waist	5
1 White messaline silk waist	7
1 White lace waist	6

1 sweater	3.5
Ruth's sweater	2.75
Marion's sweater	2.25
Richard's sweater	2
1 silk petticoat	5
6 Cambric night gowns with hand made lace	28
6 Cambric petticoats with hand made lace	20
4 Knit combinations	4
6 Cambric combinations with hand made lace	22
6 pairs stockings	1.5
1 pair shoes	4
1 pair shoes	3.5
5 pairs of gloves	10

Ruth's clothes

1 Hat	3.25
6 Cambric night gowns, trimmed hand made lace	18
1 Silk dress	5
1 Mohair dress	6
1 Linen dress	3
4 Gingham dresses	12
2 White dresses	10
1 Cloth jacket	5
6 White aprons	3
2 yards ribbon	4.8
1 Pair shoes	2.5
1 pair shoes	2
6 pairs, stockings	1.5

Marion's clothes

2 Dozen cotton dresses	24
2 Mohair dresses	6
6 Cambric undersuits	3
6 Cambric petticoats trimmed hand made lace	10
6 Night gowns	3
6 Pairs stockings	1.5
1 Pair shoes	2
6 Yards ribbon	2.4
1 White serge coat	2.5
1 Blue cloth coat	2.5
1 Tan silk coat	4.5
1 Pique jacket	2
1 Hat	2

Richard's clothes

2 Dozen cotton dresses	24
1 Mohair dress	2
1 Silk dress	3
6 Pairs stockings	1.5
1 Pair shoes	2
1 Pair shoes	2
6 Cambric petticoats	4
4 Flannel petticoats	5
12 Pairs drawers	6
4 Combination undersuits	4
2 Caps	2
6 ferris waists	1.5
6 Night gowns	4.5

Select Bibliography

Adburgham, Alison, *Shops and Shopping, 1800–1914* (Barrie & Jenkins, London, 1981).

Asquith, Cynthia, *Remember and be Glad,* (James Barrie, London, 1952).

Balsan, Consuelo Vanderbilt, *The Glitter & the Gold* (George Mann, Maidstone, 1973, (First published 1953)).

Barratt, Nick, *Lost Voices from the Titanic. The Definitive Oral History* (Preface Publishing, London, 2009).

Beveridge, Bruce, Andrews, Scott, Hall, Steve, Klistorner, Daniel, *Titanic: The Ship Magnificent, Vol 2: Interior Design & Fitting Out* (The History Press, Stroud, 2008).

Bloom, Ursula, *The Elegant Edwardian* (Hutchinson, London, 1958 (First published 1957)).

Bradfield, Nancy, *Costume in Detail, 1730–1930,* (Harrap, London, 1989).

Brogden, Anne, 'Paddy's Market', (*Costume* No. 38, 2004), pp. 106–11.

Buck, Anne, *Clothes and the Child,* (Ruth Bean, Carlton, Bedford, 1996).

Burman, Barbara, 'Home Sewing and Fashions for All, 1908–37' (*Costume* No. 28, 1994), pp. 71-80.

Byrde, Penelope, *The Twentieth Century, A Visual History of Costume,* (B. T. Batsford Ltd., London, 1986).

Carter, Alison, *Underwear, the Fashion History,* (B. T. Batsford Ltd., London, 1992).

Cooper, Diana, *The Rainbow Comes and Goes,* (Michael Russell Publishing Ltd., Salisbury, 1979, (First Published 1958)).

Cumming, Valerie, *Gloves* (B. T. Batsford Ltd., London 1982).

Duff Gordon, Lady Lucy, *Discretions & Indiscretions* (Frederick A. Stokes Company, New York, 1932).

Etherington-Smith, Meredith & Pilcher, Jeremy, *The "IT" Girls, Elinor Glyn, Novelist and her sister Lucile, Couturière* (Harcourt Brace Jovanovich, London, 1986).

Evans, Grace, 'Underwear', in Lise Skov (ed.), *Berg Encyclopedia of World Dress and Fashion, West Europe,* (Berg, Oxford and New York, 2010), pp. 389–95.

Ewing, Elizabeth, *Dress and Undress, A History of Women's Underwear,* (B. T. Batsford Ltd., London, 1986).

Ewing, Elizabeth, *History of 20th Century Fashion,* (B. T. Batsford Ltd., London, 1975).

Ewing, Elizabeth, *History of Children's Costume,* (Bibliophile, London, 1986, (First published 1977)).

Gathorne-Hardy, Jonathan, *The Rise and Fall of the British Nanny,* (Weidenfeld, London, 1993 (First published 1972)).

Geller, Judith B., *Titanic, Women & Children First* (Patrick Stephens Ltd., Yeovil, 1998).

Gernsheim, Alison, *Fashion and Reality, 1840–1914,* (Faber & Faber, London, 1963).

Ginsburg, Madeleine, 'Rags to Riches: The Second-Hand Clothes Trade 1700-1978', (*Costume* No.14, 1980), pp. 121–35.

Haas, Charles A. & Eaton, John P., *Titanic Triumph and Tragedy—a Chronicle in Words and Pictures,*

(Patrick Stephens Limited, Sparkford, 1995, (First published 1986)).

Harrison, Rosina, *Rose: My Life in Service,* (Book Club Associates, London, 1975).

Holding, T. H., *Coats,* (T. H. Holding, London, 1902).

Hyslop, Donald, Forsyth, Alastair and Jemima, Sheila, *Titanic Voices,* (Southampton City Council, 2006).

Jno. J. Mitchell Co., *Men's Fashion Illustrations from the Turn of the Century,* (Dover Publications Inc., 1990).

John Maxtone-Graham Ed., *Titanic Survivor: The Memoirs of Violet Jessop, Stewardess* (Charnwood, Leicester, 1999).

Kevill-Davies, Sally, *Yesterday's Children,* (Antique Collectors' Club, Woodbridge, 1991).

Kjellberg, Anne & North, Susan, *Style & Splendour, The Wardrobe of Queen Maud of Norway,* (V&A Publications, London, 2005).

Langbridge, R. H. (ed.), *Edwardian Shopping, A Selection from the Army & Navy Stores Catalogues, 1898–1913,* (David & Charles, London, 1975).

Lord, Walter, *A Night to Remember,* (Bantam Books, New York, 1955).

Mackrell, Alice, *Paul Poiret,* (Holmes & Meier, New York, 1990).

Mendes, Valerie & de la Haye, Amy, *Fashion since 1900,* (Thames & Hudson, London, 2010).

——*Lucile Ltd., London, Paris, New York and Chicago, 1890s–1930s,* (V&A Publishing, London, 2009).

Moore, K., *Queen Victoria is Very Ill,* (Allison & Busby Ltd., London, 1988).

Musson, Jeremy, *Up and Down Stairs, The History of the Country House Servant* (John Murray, London, 2009).

Nicholson, Juliet, *The Perfect Summer,* (John Murray, London, 2006).

Page, Christopher, *Foundations of Fashion, The Symington Collection, Corsetry from 1856 to the Present Day,* (Leicestershire Museums, 1981).

Rolley, Katrina, *Fashion in Photographs, 1900–1920,* (B. T. Batsford Ltd., London, 1992).

Sackville-West, V., *The Edwardians,* (The Hogarth Press, London, 1970 (First published 1930)).

Scarisbrick, Diana, *Jewellery,* (B. T. Batsford Ltd., London, 1984).

Seligman, Kevin L., 'Dressmakers' Patterns: The English Commercial Paper Pattern Industry, 1878–1950' (*Costume,* No. 37, 2003), pp. 95–113.

Summers, Leigh, 'Yes, They Did Wear Them: Working-Class Women and Corsetry in the Nineteenth Century', (*Costume,* No. 36, 2002), pp. 65–74.

The Lady's Realm, a selection from the monthly issues: November 1904 to April 1905 (Arrow Books Ltd., London, 1972).

The Sartorial Art Journal, Vol. XXXVIII, No 5, November 1912 (Jno. J. Mitchell Co., New York).

Vincent, W. D. F., *The Cutter's Practical Guide,* (John Williamson Co. Ltd., London, c.1904) .

Walkley, Christina & Foster, Vanda, *Crinolines and Crimping Irons, Victorian Clothes: How They were Cleaned and Cared For* (Peter Owen Ltd., London, 1978).

Waugh, Norah, *The Cut of Women's Clothes, 1600–1930* (Faber & Faber Ltd., London, 1968).

Wilcox, Claire & Mendes, Valerie, *Modern Fashion in Detail* (V&A Publications, London, 2007).

Winocour, Jack (ed.), *The Story of the Titanic as told by its Survivors* (Dover Publications Inc., New York, 1960).

Yesterday's Shopping, Gamages General Catalogue, 1914, (Wordsworth Editions, Ware, 1994).

Yesterday's Shopping, The Army & Navy Stores Catalogue, 1907, (David & Charles Reprints, 1969).

Illustration Credits

1 Portrait of Lady Duff Gordon, © National Portrait Gallery, London.

2 Lucile evening gown, © V&A Images/Victoria and Albert Museum London.

3 Two-piece tailored costume, © Royal Pavilion & Museums, Brighton & Hove.

4 Bedroom of First Class suite B60. © National Museums Northern Ireland. Collection Harland and Wolff, Ulster Folk and Transport Museum (ref: HOYFM.HW.H 1726).

5 Pair of white combinations. Image courtesy of the Olive Matthews Collection, Chertsey Museum. Photograph by John Chase (MT.2443).

6 Advertisement for the 'Spécialité Corset', The Queen, The Lady's Newspaper, March 1912. Private collection.

7 Advertisement for a corset, La Nouvelle Mode, March 1912. Private collection.

8 Advertisement for tailor-mades, The Queen, The Lady's Newspaper, March 1912. Private collection.

9 Hand-coloured fashion plate, Vrai Chic magazine, July 1910. Image courtesy of the Olive Matthews Collection, Chertsey Museum (M.1987.78.3).

10 Advertisement for a jacket, The Queen, The Lady's Newspaper, March 1912. Private collection.

11 Two First Class passengers on Titanic's Promenade. © Father Francis M. Browne. S. J. Collection.

12 Three women's hats. Image courtesy of the Olive Matthews Collection, Chertsey Museum. Photographs by John Chase (M.2006.04-06).

13 Pair of long black gloves. Image courtesy of the Olive Matthews Collection, Chertsey Museum (M.1997.7).

14 Advertisement for an ostrich feather hat, The Queen, The Lady's Newspaper, March 1912. Private collection.

15 Advertisement for hair pieces, The Queen, The Lady's Newspaper, March 1912. Private collection.

16 Advertisement for a Burberry topcoat, The Queen, The Lady's Newspaper, March 1912. Private collection.

17 The First Class gymnasium.© National Museums Northern Ireland. Collection Harland and Wolff, Ulster Folk and Transport Museum (ref: HOYFM.HW.H 1730).

18 Mr Lawrence Beesley in Titanic's gymnasium. Image courtesy of Mary Evans Picture Library.

19 Artist's impression of the swimming bath on board Titanic. Image courtesy of Mary Evans Picture Library.

20 First Class Café Parisien on Titanic's B deck. © National Museums Northern Ireland. Collection Harland and Wolff, Ulster Folk and Transport Museum (ref: HOYFM.HW.H 1733).

21 First Class reading and writing room. © National Museums Northern Ireland. Collection Harland and Wolff, Ulster Folk and Transport Museum (ref: HOYFM.HW.H 1841).

22 The First Class dining saloon on *Olympic*. *The Shipbuilder* magazine, Special Number 1911. Private collection.

23 Designs for day wear, *Supplement au Messager des Modes*. Image courtesy of the Olive Matthews Collection, Chertsey Museum (M.1987.78.1).

25 Black tea-gown. Image courtesy of the Olive Matthews Collection, Chertsey Museum. Photograph by John Chase (M.1998.49).

26 Artist's drawing of the First Class elevator on *Olympic*. *The Shipbuilder* magazine, Special Number 1911. Private collection.

27 Examples of hair styles, *The Queen, The Lady's Newspaper*, March 1912. Private collection.

28 Design for an evening gown, *Supplement au Messager des Modes*, February 1910. Image courtesy of the Olive Matthews Collection, Chertsey Museum (M.1987.78.8).

29 An evening ensemble, © V&A Images/Victoria and Albert Museum London.

30 Satin evening gown. Images courtesy of the Olive Matthews Collection, Chertsey Museum. Photographs by John Chase (M.1997.14).

31 Evening coat. Images courtesy of the Olive Matthews Collection, Chertsey Museum. Photographs by John Chase (M.2006.09).

32 Verandah and Palm court, *Olympic*. *The Shipbuilder* magazine, Special Number 1911. Private collection.

33 Liberty Bodice. Images courtesy of Leicestershire Museums Service.

34 Miss Freda Gray. Image courtesy of Chertsey Museum (CHYMS.2829.9).

35 Small girl's coat. Image courtesy of Chertsey Museum (M.1994.4).

36 Silk knitted gloves. Image courtesy of the Olive Matthews Collection, Chertsey Museum (M.2003.04).

37 Child's leather boots. Image courtesy of the Olive Matthews Collection, Chertsey Museum (M.1992.4).

38 Boy's cotton dress. Images courtesy of the Olive Matthews Collection, Chertsey Museum (M.2001.21)

39 Boy's sailor suit. Image courtesy of the Olive Matthews Collection, Chertsey Museum (M.1998.1).

40 Advertisement for tunic suits, *The Queen,*

The Lady's Newspaper, March 1912. Private collection.

41 An Eton suit from T. H. Holding, Coats, 1902. Private Collection.

42 Fashions for girls, *Supplement au Vrai Chic...* , July 1910. Image courtesy of the Olive Matthews Collection, Chertsey Museum (M.1987.78.7).

43 Harrods advertisement, *The Queen, The Lady's Newspaper*, March 1912. Private collection.

44 Bedroom of First Class suite, B57, on *Titanic*. © National Museums Northern Ireland. Collection Harland and Wolff, Ulster Folk and Transport Museum (ref: HOYFM.HW.H 1724).

45 Morning Dress, from T. H. Holding, *Coats*, 1902. Private Collection.

46 Men's lounge suits, *Sartorial Art Journal*, June 1904. Image courtesy of Dover Publications, Inc.

47 Man's lounge suit. Image courtesy of the Olive Matthews Collection, Chertsey Museum. Photograph by John Chase (M.1991.7).

48 Man's bowler hat. Image courtesy of the Olive Matthews Collection, Chertsey Museum (M.1987.88).

49 Men's overcoats, *Sartorial Art Journal*, December 1909. Image courtesy of Dover Publications, Inc.

50 Man in a racing punt. Image courtesy of Chertsey Museum (CHYMS.0919.3).

51 Men's evening dress, *Sartorial Art Journal*, November 1904. Image courtesy of Dover Publications, Inc.

52 Men's evening dress, *Sartorial Art Journal*, December 1905. Image courtesy of Dover Publications, Inc.

53 Smoking jacket, from T. H. Holding, *Coats*, 1902. Private collection.

54 The First Class smoking room on board *Olympic*, *The Shipbuilder* magazine, Special Number 1911.

55 Artist's impression of the Second Class promenade. Image courtesy of Mary Evans Picture Library.

56 Artist's impression of a Second Class cabin. Image courtesy of Mary Evans Picture Library.

57 Second Class library on *Olympic*, *The Shipbuilder* magazine, Special Number 1911. Private collection.

58 Artist's impression of the Third Class smoking room on board *Titanic*. Image courtesy of Mary Evans Picture Library.

59 A Sunday School outing. Image courtesy of Chertsey Museum (CHYMS.2005.026.1).
60 Enjoying a day of sport. Image courtesy of Chertsey Museum (CHYMS.3829.104).
61 Cover of French fashion magazine *La Nouvelle Mode*. Private collection.
62 A Jenyns corset. Images courtesy of Leicestershire Museums Service.
63 Advertisement for paper pattern, *The Queen, The Lady's Newspaper*, March 1912. Private collection.
64 Advertisement for 'Parisian shoes', *The Queen, The Lady's Newspaper*, March 1912. Private collection.
65 Lace-up shoes and boots. Image courtesy of the Olive Matthews Collection, Chertsey Museum (M.2006.29 and M.1992.4)
66 An infant school class. Image courtesy of Chertsey Museum (CHYMS.2010.020.141).
67 Family group. Image courtesy of Chertsey Museum (CHYMS.3829/114).

68 Replica of cap badge. Private collection.
69 Bill from Miller's Naval Tailors and Outfitters. Image courtesy of Southampton City Heritage Collections.
70 Officer's jacket. Courtesy National Museums Liverpool.
71 Captain Edward J. Smith and officers. Image courtesy of Mary Evans Picture Library.
72 Crew loading mail sacks. © Father Francis M. Browne. S. J. Collection.
73 Maids. Image courtesy of Chertsey Museum (CHYMS.2007.065.2).
74 Advertisements for luggage, *Illustrated London News*, July 1, 1911. Image courtesy of Special Collections, Cadbury Research Library, University of Birmingham.
75 Advertisement for trunk, *Guide through Europe*, Hamburg-Amerika Line, 1914, Private collection.
76 Apron worn by Miss Francatelli. Courtesy National Museums Liverpool.